GRITTY
FRIENDSHIPS

GRITTY
FRIENDSHIPS

BRINGING PURPOSE
AND VALUE TO
MALE RELATIONSHIPS

DR CARLYLE SNIDER NAYLOR

Copyright © 2024 by Dr Carlyle Snider Naylor

All rights reserved. No part of this book may be used or reproduced in any manner whatsoever without prior written consent of the author, except as provided by the United States of America copyright law.

Published by Best Seller Publishing®, St. Augustine, FL
Best Seller Publishing® is a registered trademark.
Printed in the United States of America.

ISBN: 978-1-962595-10-0

This publication is designed to provide accurate and authoritative information with regard to the subject matter covered. It is sold with the understanding that the publisher is not engaged in rendering legal, accounting, or other professional advice. If legal advice or other expert assistance is required, the services of a competent professional should be sought. The opinions expressed by the author in this book are not endorsed by Best Seller Publishing® and are the sole responsibility of the author rendering the opinion.

For more information, please write:
Best Seller Publishing®
1775 US-1 #1070
St. Augustine, FL 32084
or call 1 (626) 765-9750
Visit us online at: www.BestSellerPublishing.org

The information contained in this book is informational only and does not constitute legal advice or an offer to sell you a franchise. Please make sure to do thorough due diligence before investing in any franchise or business opportunity and always consult the services of an experienced franchise attorney.

This book is dedicated to the gritty
Man I love the most - Jesus Christ.

And to the gritty and girly woman I love the most - Tina.

And to the gritty men that have made
me a gritty friend over the years.

And to Jon, the gritty man whose life and death
inspired me to write about gritty friendships - and
to his family, the Kempiak Party of 5.

This book was great. Carlyle gives real helpful tools for us dudes. As someone who at times neglects deeper male relationships, I felt encouraged and nudged to act. It will also come in very handy for the men's group I facilitate. I highly recommend it. Thanks Carlyle.

— Charlie Boeyink

This book got to me right away. As a female and an older adult, it was not geared towards me, but it spoke to me immediately as it can be for everyone who wants, has, or is a friend. I hope men of all ages will read this book, but especially older men, and will follow the guidelines of being a friend. My generation was not taught how to be friends, especially men who have fended for themselves in relationships. I want to thank Dr Naylor for reaching out to other men and guiding them in the closeness of friendships.

— Cynthia Bartelone

As a man who has benefitted from a gritty relationship with Carlyle for nearly 20 years, reading this book helped me understand the method to some of his madness. During those years of Friday morning coffees with Carlyle and a few other buddies, we laughed at stupid jokes and were often driven to action by Carlyle's challenging probes into our relatively mundane life issues. Now that I am entering the retirement years of my life, I see the blessing his gritty friendship has been to my spiritual journey, my family, and my career. I highly recommend this book to any man who wants to challenge himself and others to do more than "get through life"! And the last chapter...it was very moving.

— Byron Dixon

Why do men hesitate to invest the same level of dedication and intentionality in their friendships as they do in their careers and families? Dr. Naylor delves into the unique dynamics of male friendships and provides concrete recommendations on how to develop and cultivate meaningful long-term relationships that foster genuine connection.

— Tom LaVelle

Carlyle has been a guiding influence for me and my family as we've journeyed through our spiritual beliefs. His guidance has been invaluable in shaping me into a better Christian man for my wife and kids. Now, I'm grateful that his wisdom is extending beyond our home to help me become a better man for my community. This book holds the same potential for every man who picks it up, offering valuable insights and guidance for personal growth. I'm thrilled that Carlyle has shared his wisdom in a book accessible to everyone, making it easier for others to benefit from his teachings.

— Scott Barlow

I was truly inspired by Dr. Carlyle Naylor's book "Gritty Friendships". The book emphasizes the importance of men's deep, meaningful relationships, and provides easy-to-follow steps on how to develop gritty friendships. As a woman, I found the stories shared within the book were deep and powerful, and I believe that anyone who reads it will gain an understanding of the significance of deep "gritty" friendships. This would be great for a men's small group study as Dr. Naylor also brings in biblical applications throughout the book. I'm excited to gift this book to my husband, as I'm sure he will benefit greatly from it, and I hope that others will be inspired to deepen and improve their friendships as well!

— Autumn Sandquist

In this day and age of technology, men are bombarded with simulacra posing as hyper-real, "better than reality" false promises making it easier than ever to isolate. Naylor brings a refreshing reminder that real friendship between men is not only better but seriously necessary. He tackles tough topics, that we as men might not want to admit, while offering real-life examples, humor, and wisdom from his own experiences. Honest, relatable, and so much more than just a self help book. All men, whether you're struggling or not, need this book so we can start living our legacy now.

— Brandon Camping

Practical. Relational. Transparent. Timely. Biblical. Dr. Naylor (or "Pastor C", as my wife, kids and I know him) writes Gritty Friendships, a primer for guys on male relationships, with extremely practical, relational, transparent, and timely wisdom from a biblical and pastoral perspective. He is one of the most relational men you will every meet. Relationships mean everything to Pastor C. So, it's no surprise that he has given his life to counseling people in them; whether from the pulpit, in a small group or one-on-one. Gritty Friendships challenged me and will challenge you to prioritize, value, and cultivate the relationships we have and desperately need with other men. With decades of experience as a pastor and life coach, Dr. Naylor's professional study and personal observations an insights show up on every page. One of my favorite, and the most challenging parts, are the poignant questions at the end of each chapter. They help apply the content personally. Page 49 is the best!

— Joel N. Thurston, Esq.

Dr. Naylor does a tremendous job of marrying up a lifetime of experiences as a pastor and relationship coach with the grittiness of men desiring, but struggling with, how to develop close relationships with other men. Gritty Friendships is a light read but packs a punch, providing real-life examples backed by tons of research with practical and easy to steps that will help all men not only take the first step into discovering the power of "gritty" relationships, but will help with developing those relationships to be life-transforming.

— Chris Ritchie

I really enjoyed this book. A brilliant mixture of personal antidotes, experienced research from numerous sources, and accurate citations. Dr. Naylor is building his legacy as an impacting writer in my humble opinion.

— Torrey D. Naylor

*True friendship multiplies the good
in life and divides its evils.*

— Baltasar Gracian - Mid 17th Century
Jesuit Writer/Philosopher

Friendship is the hardest thing in the world to explain. It's not something you learn in school. But if you haven't learned the meaning of friendship, you really haven't learned anything.

— Muhammad Ali - Late 20th Century
American Professional Boxer

Contents

1. Gritty Isolation 1
2. Gritty Initiative 19
3. Gritty Experiences 39
4. Gritty Conversations 57
5. Gritty Habits 79
6. Gritty Accountability 101
7. Gritty Emotional Intelligence 125
8. Gritty Longevity 147
9. Gritty Legacy 169

CHAPTER 1: GRITTY ISOLATION

Aloneness is different from loneliness. Unfortunately the stats tell us that men suffer from both, and both are detrimental to the masculine soul. This chapter appeals to men who have reached the point where they realize they need deeper, grittier friendships in their lives, yet are hesitant about, or don't know how to go about, creating these kinds of friendships.

CHAPTER 2: GRITTY INITIATIVE

Striving is a relevant part of a man's DNA. But typical male striving leaves men lesser than they were meant to be because of a lack of meaningful masculine relationships. Most men are waiting for some other guy to take the first step into meaningful male friendships - which leaves a bunch of men just waiting around. This chapter offers 5 easy and repeatable steps to take the friendship initiative.

CHAPTER 3: GRITTY EXPERIENCES

We all live for experiences these days. Men always have! We don't have to recreate experiences, just recalibrate ones that already exist. This chapter taps 5 ways men can take some of the common interests already present in male friendships to make them meaningful and impacting beyond the experience.

CHAPTER 4: GRITTY CONVERSATIONS

There are a lot of moving parts in a man's life. Focusing on the things that really matter make life and relationships matter. Surface conversations never get a man to what matters. This chapter explores how to positively access the "negativity bias" to reframe masculine realities with 5 elements of a meaningful conversation.

CHAPTER 5: GRITTY HABITS

We all have them - even if we don't remember where they came from. We have habits we are proud of and others that are hidden in shame. This chapter will help men explore 5 elements of good habits that can help transform the mind, soul and body.

CHAPTER 6: GRITTY ACCOUNTABILITY

Humans, left to themselves, have the uncanny ability to sabotage things that are really in their best interest. Men especially have the passive tendency to self-sabotage. Personal isolation will alway lead to personal desolation, but male-to-male accountability is an easy and sustainable antidote to self-sabotage. This chapter unpacks an easy 6-part formula for meaningful accountability.

CHAPTER 7: GRITTY EMOTIONAL INTELLIGENCE

Intelligence is the acquisition and application of relevant information. Emotional intelligence is the same thing, but is exclusively applied to relationships. Too many men are emotionally ignorant and emotionally incontinent. But there's hope! This chapter explores how men can decode the emotional man-code by applying 3 essential components of emotional awareness and management.

CHAPTER 8: GRITTY LONGEVITY

The pathways of too many men are strewn with too many dead male friendships because of neglect and inconsistency. Why do men struggle to sustain long-term male relationships? This chapter borrows "mental toughness" as a way to develop "friendship toughness" to regain and sustain long-term, meaningful male friendships.

CHAPTER 9: GRITTY LEGACY

One day, maybe all too soon, all men will ask themselves how their life actually mattered. Men's need for legacy is closely related to their masculinity and their God-given purpose. The book ends with a call to engage purposeful legacy-making through 4 easy legacy capstones that will outlive you! The chapter ends with a full-circle surprise story connected to the opening story.

1
Gritty Isolation

"Jon died." There was more to the text message than that, but those were the only words I could take in before my head started to spin.

This was a summer day in Phoenix, 2016. The text was from Carol, the mother of my friend Jon Kempiak. Wanting to read the whole message in private, I slipped out of the coffeehouse, where I had been waiting for an appointment, and went to my car. There I read the rest of the text: "Jon died from a massive heart attack this morning. They are visiting California. I have no details".

As hot as it was that day, I started shaking as if I were freezing.

What? This can't be. It doesn't make sense. Jon? No.

Jon was forty-six years old. He had a wife, Kymberly, and three children. He was a successful account rep for a software company; he had more friends than most of us could imagine having; and he was full of life and plans for the future. He couldn't just be...gone.

But he was. As I learned later, he had simply fallen dead from an undetected heart condition, right in front of his wife and kids while they were on vacation.

After taking a few minutes to absorb the news of Jon's death, I called Kymberly. The call went to her voicemail. I tried to keep my voice calm as I told her I would drop everything and drive to her and the kids immediately if she needed me to. Then I hung up, sat in my car, and cried. Actually, what was coming out of me was more like a sob than a cry, the type that comes from your gut, that shakes your core.

But here's the curious thing—the depth of my response confused me. As much as I loved my friend Jon, we had grown apart over the years leading up to his death. Why was I so wracked by the news of his unexpected death?

My mind inevitably went back to how we met and how we got close.

A FRIENDSHIP THAT FADED...BUT NEVER ENDED

Jon and I became friends when we were both part of a team starting a church together—me as one of the pastors and he as the volunteer music/worship director. We started meeting weekly for coffee and conversation.

It wasn't long before we got to deep issues regarding our spirituality, our marriages, our careers, leadership, masculinity, sexuality—no issue was off limits. Some of these topics were hard to address. Some of them were easy. All of our conversations were empowering.

Jon and I also got together occasionally to do things we both enjoyed. For example, we got into mountain biking together, eating out at restaurants, and discussing books.

The two couples also got close. We spent most holidays together. Jon and I went on frequent double dates with our wives, even traveling together for weekend trips. The four of us were unstoppable at Disneyland.

After a few years, though, my wife and I moved ten miles away to start another church. Because of this move, and because of challenging and busy schedules, a gap appeared in my friendship with Jon. Soon our times together evaporated altogether, though the four of us, as couples, still got together once a year or so. We tried to share milestones with each other, such as the births of their three children, decade birthday celebrations, and the like. I never stopped caring for Jon, but our friendship was nothing like it had been. Here are some sequential pictures from early in our relationship (top, left) to a few months before I got that message from Jon's mom (bottom, right). Jon always had less hair on his head than I did, but he wore it well!

Jon's death made me realize how much I still cared about him. It also showed me how important male friendships are—or should be. I'd had friendships with other men before I met Jon, and I continued to have such friendships after Jon and I drifted apart, but none of them were as close and meaningful as my friendship with Jon. When he died, I realized that my only really close male friend was gone.

I felt lonely.

Sadly, that meant I was part of a very large club.

AN EPIDEMIC AND ITS COSTS

Loneliness is a modern-day epidemic. A survey from 2020 (taken before coronavirus restrictions forced many of us to stay home that year) revealed that 61 percent of Americans felt lonely—a 7 percent increase just since 2018.[1]

With loneliness so common, you might conclude we as humans are wired for loneliness. But really we are wired for connection, and we have been since the very beginning.

In the creation story, Adam does the work God equipped him to do, naming the animals. But in doing this Adam noticed something was lacking. Every animal had another animal of its kind; Adam didn't. It was at that time, in God's love and compassion for Adam, that he created Eve. She would enhance Adam's quality of life in all its realms—physical, emotional, and spiritual.

Marriage isn't the only relationship that can meet our need to know and be known. In fact, it takes many kinds of same, and cross-gender, relationships to have the richest life of community with others.

But if we are created for relationships, why are we so lonely?

One factor is that people have only a limited number of relational hooks. That means they have the capacity to have only a few close relationships because of constraints on their time, their emotions, or their initiative.

A popular anthropologist, Robin Dunbar, has a theory that the human brain is capable of keeping track of only about 150 relationships—people that we know enough to care about them in some capacity. Of those 150, only 50 of them are people that

---

[1] Cigna Insurance, news release, "Cigna Takes Action to Combat the Rise of Loneliness and Improve Mental Wellness in America," January 23, 2020,
https://www.cigna.com/about-us/newsroom/news-and-views/press-releases/2020/cigna-takes-action-to-combat-the-rise-of-loneliness-and-improve-mental-wellness-in-america

are likely closer to us— that we would hang out with or have over to our house. Of those 50, we will likely be even closer to 15 of them. And it gets smaller and more exclusive. Of those 15, only 5 of them will really know us and us them. We will share up to 50 percent of our social time with these 5, and these are the ones we call in some kind of crisis.[2] Unfortunately, the crisis is usually something like a flat tire when our AAA has expired, not a crisis of identity, insecurity, or fear.

We have limited capacity for each level of relationship, and most of us don't even come close to that capacity. And consequently, without reaching our human potential for friendship, we get lonely.

This is not just an unfortunate outcome. It's dangerous. Consider these facts.

- Loneliness increases the likelihood of mortality by 26 percent.
- The effect of loneliness and isolation on mortality is comparable to the impact of well-known risk factors such as obesity, and it has a similar influence as cigarette smoking.
- Loneliness is associated with an increased risk of developing coronary heart disease and stroke.
- Loneliness increases the risk of high blood pressure.
- Loneliness puts individuals at greater risk of cognitive decline and dementia.
- Lonely individuals are more prone to depression.
- Loneliness and low social interaction are predictive of suicide.[3]

---

[2] Christine Rho, Dunbar's Number: Why We Can Only Maintain 150 Relationships. BBC Future, October 9, 2019. https://www.bbc.com/future/article/20191001-dunbars-number-why-we-can-only-maintain-150-relationships

[3] Campaign to End Loneliness, https://www.campaigntoendloneliness.org/threat-to-health/

Loneliness is serious business. I think you won't be surprised to learn that this problem is even greater for men than for women.

A GUY'S PROBLEM

While many women seem to naturally form friendships with other women, men—not so much.

Study after study shows that men are lonelier than women. A 2011 study found that male university students were significantly more likely to report feelings of loneliness than female students. A 2018 analysis of people living in rural regions found that 63 percent of men felt comfortable opening up to friends, compared to 74 percent of women. Women were also more likely to participate in activities, such as church gatherings, that foster friendship and a sense of community.[4] White heterosexual men have the fewest friends of anyone in America.[5]

Not only do men have fewer friendships, but also those friendships tend to be less personal. According to a study in a scientific journal, whereas women favor one-to-one interactions, male friendships are more likely to flourish in groups.[6] And as one investigator into male loneliness said, "When men do get together, it is still often to watch sports, or, if their muscles

---

[4] Studies cited in Zawn Villines, "Life as a Lone Wolf: Why Do So Many Men Feel Lonely?" December 9, 2019, GoodTherapy, https://www.goodtherapy.org/blog/life-as-lone-wolf-why-do-so-many-men-feel-lonely-129197.

[5] Miller McPherson, Lynn Smith-Lovin and Matthew E. Brashears, "Social Isolation in America: Changes in Core Discussion Networks over Two Decades," American Sociological Review 71, no. 3 (June 2006), 353-375.

[6] Tamas David Barrett and others, "Women Favour Dyadic Relationships, but Men Prefer Clubs: Cross-Cultural Evidence from Social Networking," PLOS One, March 16, 2015, https://doi.org/10.1371/journal.pone.0118329.

haven't atrophied, to engage in them."[7] In active groups, men are less likely to share the deep-seated issues of their lives.

Josh Glancy experienced loneliness when he moved to a new city, and since he was a journalist, he started studying the phenomenon of loneliness. He concluded, "Loneliness isn't gendered, but men in particular tend to struggle to express deep feelings and form meaningful connections. Many of us find it easier to talk about football or politics than to admit to suffering from a low sex drive or feeling undervalued at work. We don't know who to tell these things, or how to say them."[8]

Even worse, lately there seems to be a trend of masculine friendships straying away from group activities and moving toward isolationism. Many men are "bowling alone," as one US political scientist, Robert D. Putnam, put it in his book by the same title.[9] People are taking up more activities, but they are doing it alone rather than with teams or leagues or other groups. Here there isn't even a semblance of friendships. We've gone from "weism" to "meism," and we're paying the price.[10]

Yet many men I know yearn for one-on-one friendships with other guys. I've had men tell me that they have never experienced a male friendship that went to a deep and meaningful level. They've been lonely most of their lives.

I made a new friend this year. He is sharp, smart, articulate, and deep. But I could see that he was lonely. I reached out to him. We hit it off quickly, mostly because I asked him about

---

[7] Michele Willens, "The Challenges and Rewards of Male-on-Male Friendship," The Atlantic, January 17, 2013, https://www.theatlantic.com/sexes/archive/2013/01/the-challenges-and-rewards-of-male-on-male-friendship/267284/.

[8] Josh Glancy, "The Uncomfortable Truth about Male Loneliness," Men's Health, May 2, 2019, https://www.menshealth.com/uk/mental-strength/a759609/the-truth-about-male-loneliness/.

[9] Robert D. Putnam, Bowling Alone: The Collapse and Revival of American Community, rev. ed. (New York : Simon & Schuster, 2020).

[10] Robert D. Putnam, The Upswing: How America Came Together a Century Ago and How We Can Do It Again (New York : Simon & Schuster, 2020).

some important things that really mattered to him–some hard parenting issues he was going through.

He said, "I have never had a friend like you before."

Another man I have been having coffee with every week for fifteen years said almost the same thing. "You reached out to me—your pursued me. No one else had really done that before—ever."

As Brett McKay, who runs The Art of Manliness website, says, "Most adult men very much want good friends but just don't know how to make them."[11]

Meanwhile, the significant women in men's lives want them to have male friendships. It's not just that a lonely man's wife, girlfriend, or mom feels sorry for him and wants him to be happier and more fulfilled by having at least one strong male friendship. It's also that a man's lack of male friendship can place a burden on the women in his life. As one couples therapy specialist noted, "Men who do not have male friends often rely too much on their women and expect too much from them."[12]

The reasons men are lonelier than women are varied. Many guys fall into the trap of focusing on their families, careers, possessions, and financial balances to the exclusion of more important things, especially as they enter middle age. They just don't take time for friendship with other guys, because it's not a high priority. But also I think many men perceive friendship as a feminine thing—it's for the gender that tends to be better at emotions and relationships. Even if they want male friendships, men think they don't know how and are hesitant to try.

---

[11] Brett McKay, interview with Geoffrey Greif, "Understanding Male Friendships," podcast 360, The Art of Manliness, https://www.artofmanliness.com/articles/understanding-male- friendships/.

[12] Psychiatrist Dr. John Jacobs, quoted in Michele Willens, "The Challenges and Rewards of Male-on-Male Friendship," The Atlantic, January 17, 2013, https://www.theatlantic.com/sexes/archive/2013/01/the-challenges-and-rewards-of-male-on- male-friendship/267284/.

In a HuffPost article, Brittany Wong wrote:

Research shows that men are just as likely as women to say they want emotional intimacy in their friendships. But as many a think piece has suggested, our ideas about masculinity are at odds with that: A boy approaching adulthood is expected to be stoic, to stifle his feelings and bottle up any complicated emotions.

Manhood, we're told, leaves little room for the kind of emotional intimacy friendship requires. But men crave that closeness—even those who do have friends say they wouldn't mind being closer with them, said Robert Garfield, a psychotherapist and the author of "Breaking the Male Code: Unlocking the Power of Friendship."[13]

Fear of Vulnerability

Another reason men are missing out on male friendship is good old-fashioned fear of being vulnerable. Men are taught often and early that vulnerability is not a safe place for males. Vulnerability puts your burden on someone else. Men are supposed to carry their own burdens—pain and isolation and all.[14]

This is contrary to what most men experience when they are vulnerable with a friend. Think back yourself to a time when you shared something with a male friend that raised your blood pressure a little when you shared it. Did your friend "peace out" on you, leaving the room awkwardly and then canceling your next gym session together? Most of the time men discover that

---

[13] Brittany Wong, "Are Men Really Having a 'Friendship Crisis,'" Huffington Post, November 6, 2019, https://www.huffpost.com/entry/men-friendship-crisis_l_5dbc9aa7e4b0576b62a1e90f.

[14] Maija Kappler, "Navigating: Why Is It Hard for Men to Make Friends?" Huffington Post, July 28, 2019, https://www.huffingtonpost.ca/entry/how-to-make-friends-men-navigating_ca_5d39ff76e4b020cd99509ab1.

they are going through similar things with similar reactions. There is more of a camaraderie than a rejection.

Fear of Rejection

Men and women are different in the way they respond to rejection, real or perceived. Women take rejection more as a personal affront. Men take it more as a social affront.

Men and women respond [to rejection] differently in culturally normative ways: Males tend to take rejection as a challenge to their masculinity or an insult to their perceived place in the social hierarchy. Women are likely to feel emotionally hurt by a rejection and to assume that there is something lacking in them that warranted the rejection or blame the person who did the rejecting but use self-soothing to get over the insult rather than lashing out as males might do. Women are encouraged to "get over it," but men often feel the need to "get even."[15]

As a result of men's reactions to the affront of rejection, they affront back. They strike out with subtle and obvious attacks that continue the cycle of rejection—eliminating the possibility of a close connection with each psychological, emotional, and verbal affront. If you don't think this is true, take an honest step back and listen to men talk about other men when they are not present.

A GUY'S SOLUTION

Do close friendships, where men discuss their deep issues, detract from manliness?

---

[15] Suzanne Degges-White, "Rejection: Why It Hurt Men More than It Should," Psychology Today, May 24, 2018, https://www.psychologytoday.com/us/blog/lifetime- connections/201805/rejection-when-it-hurts-men-more-it-should.

Here's what I have to say about that: *Absolutely not. Deep friendships aren't just for women. They aren't superfluous. Meaningful male friendships are in fact the missing link to a fulfilled male life—helping men be all they can be!*

I don't think it's just me who is looking for the kinds of things I gained from spending time with Jon. An opportunity to relax and be myself. A recovery of the lightheartedness I'd enjoyed about myself as a boy. Reassurance that I wasn't alone. A fresh perspective on my problems and new ideas for what to do about them. More confidence that I have the courage and strength to be a leader. More honesty about my doubts and insecurities. More courage to face my giants—large and small. More strength to step into things with confidence and appropriate bravado.

A better man, in other words. A better me.

If you're a man who desires more and better friendships with other guys, let me assure you that deep male friendships not only are more doable and more comfortable than you may have assumed but can actually make you into a better and more manly man in your life as a husband, father, worker, and leader.

Let me describe one small but representative way that happened in my own life. Once again, it goes back to my friend Jon Kempiak.

LESSON FINALLY LEARNED

The first road trip I ever took with a male friend was with Jon, back when we were living near each other and getting together regularly. As I've said, we had gotten into mountain biking together. Our bikes barely qualified as mountain bikes, but we rode them on difficult trails because we didn't know any better.

We had fun with it anyway. Our motto became "If we don't puke or bleed, it wasn't a good ride." In fact, we enjoyed our local rides so much that we decided to go on a trip to a mountain town to camp and ride.

On that trip, the conversation, the scenery, and the bike riding were all great. So were the inch-and-a-half New York steaks that I had especially butcher-cut for our trip. But none of those things are what I remember most about the trip.

Because of a missing gasket on the radiator cap, my truck kept overheating as we made our way up the curvy mountain road that led to our camping area. So we had to stop to let the truck cool down. There we were, weaving our way up and out of the Salt River Canyon in the middle of the White River Apache Reservation of Arizona, looking down on a stream falling through red rocks of a gorge, with junipers and piñons clinging to the hillsides. What did we do while we waited? We threw rocks of course.

Even though Jon was skinny, artistic, musical, and sensitive, he was also masculine. He knew how to throw. He started grabbing rocks and throwing them, telling me in advance what he was aiming for. "Okay, Carlyle, see that stump there by the boulder? I'm going to hit that." And sure enough, he hit the stump.

I watched and appreciated.

"You throw one," he said after a while.

That's what I'd been afraid he would say.

Here's the problem. When I was growing up, I was raised by the man my mother married. We struggled to connect, and as a consequence, he never spent much time teaching me how to throw things like baseballs—or rocks. So I grew up without being able to throw hard, accurately, or with any finesse.

When Jon invited me to throw rocks with him, I didn't want him to see how unmanly I was, as evidenced by awkward, haphazard, and spastic rock throwing.

"No thanks. I'm not very good."

"Oh, come on. That doesn't matter."

He finally persuaded me to join him in target practice. I threw badly, but Jon didn't care about that. He encouraged me and gave me advice on throwing.

"Try it more side arm. Keep your eye on the target. That's right."

I tried again.

The overheating truck forced us to stop several times along the side of the road. So we kept on throwing rocks. And Jon's persistence and encouragement finally resulted in my picking off targets and aiming at farther rocks and bushes.

A guy who knew a lot about being a friend, Jon gently encouraged me to do something I felt insecure about. He placed no judgment on my perceived lack of masculinity or on my rock-throwing disability. So I grew in boldness. After a few stops, I was looking forward to the next target practice.

That was how our relationship worked. We encouraged each other. We challenged each other. We probed into the deeper part of our mannish souls. Our wives loved the relationship we had, because they thought we were better men because of each other. And it was true. We had a gritty relationship.

LIVING LEGACY

Jon's funeral was standing room only. Literally, people were standing in the lobby because every other inch of space was taken by people sitting and standing in the church auditorium.

I got to speak at his funeral. As I stood at the lectern, I was able to see the faces and body language of hundreds of people. I was struck by the pain people were exhibiting. Some of the pain came from all of us seeing his wife and three kids struggling to get through the funeral with dignity. But I also saw men—hundreds of men—who had experienced a taste of what Jon and I had experienced with each other. You see, I was far from Jon's only male friend. In the course of his adult life, he'd kept up with an amazing number of friendships. Real friendships that changed hearts and minds and behaviors in positive ways.

I jokingly say in my career as a pastor and life coach that when I make a grown man cry, I have done my job well. Jon did his job well that day. Man after man got up, with teary eyes and shaky voices, and shared how Jon's friendship and influence had changed them.

I saw the devastation of isolation that day, because men had lost a friend. I heard it in the voices of the men who rose from their seats to share about Jon and his influence on them. I saw it in the eyes of men who couldn't stand and speak but "spoke" with their body language as they sat in silence. I also saw fear that day—a fear that what they saw in Jon and experienced through him was a one-time shot. I think they thought their chance at gritty male friendship was over.

It wasn't.

It's not.

Two weeks after Jon died, one of his coworkers, who was at Jon's funeral, called me. His name was Reggie. We exchanged a few emails and set up a time to drink coffee together. When we met, we made some small talk about their working relationship. Quickly, he got around to his point.

"I want my life to be more like Jon's," he said.

"In what way?"

"Well, you saw how many guys Jon kept in touch with. He had a life of meaning and connection."

We decided to keep meeting. He joined one of my men's groups. He and I would meet for an hour first, then the rest of the group would come.

Our conversations, and the group conversation, led to a faith experience for him. Seeing Jon's impact, and then experiencing it firsthand in our group, made him curious for the faith that Jon and the rest of us had. So he took a step of faith at one of our pre-meetings. He became a Christian.

As a pastor, I was elated.

As a friend, I was humbled.

As Jon's friend, I was blown away by Jon's legacy.

Moments after his experience, I snapped a picture of Reggie and sent it to Jon's widow with the caption "This is Reggie. He just had a personal encounter with Jesus and took a step of faith to believe in him. This is your husband's legacy."

She was stunned with joy. She actually couldn't even text me back for about an hour because she was so emotionally moved. Jon was still dead, but he was living on in front of her eyes.

The depth and meaning Jon and I experienced with each other had kept going. Between the two of us, we had the privilege and honor of befriending literally hundreds of men in meaningful relationships that changed both them and us.

After Jon died, I decided to fight the male tendency of slinking into isolation. I was going to make time for the things that matter most to me: relationships. Primarily my relationship with my wonderful wife, but also the friendships I hoped to form with other men. I was going to help create a movement, small or large, of men coming alongside other men. I wanted to help men have gritty relationships that would change things for them before they got a text that their friend was dead.

This was our last get-together with Jon and Kymberly - a few months before Jon unexpectedly died.

THE MOVEMENT

This book is for men who have reached the point where they realize they need deeper, grittier friendships in their lives, yet are hesitant about, or don't know how to go about, creating these kinds of friendships. And it is for women who want to help the men in their lives to have deeper friendships. (To these women I would say, read this book and then pass it along to a friendship-starved man.)

Thanks to Jon's example, today I have strong friendships with other men. I'll be telling about many of the experiences I've had with them, just as I've told about some of my experiences with Jon.

I want you to learn how to have the same kinds of friendships. Not just the kind of relationship where you can say, "Hey, bro, wanna come to the game with me?" But the kind of relationship where you can talk about things that matter. It's about getting to know each other in a safe but deep way. And helping each other.

This kind of friendship doesn't make you less of a man. It makes you more of a man. You and your friend can make each other braver—with more courage to try new things, face hard truths, and become proactive. You can make each other stronger—better equipped to deal with life's challenges, more confident, more resilient.

Make some friends. Encourage those friends to make some friends. And it can multiply from there. Maybe together we can reverse the trend of lonely and isolated men.

Just as a sports team uses a playbook to carry out a strategy for a game, this book provides you with eight "plays" that, if carried out well and in sequence, will create a "win" in male friendship.

DISCUSSION QUESTIONS

1. In what ways have you felt lonely recently? Did you keep this to yourself?
2. Do any of the stories in this chapter grab you? How does it stir you up?
3. Do you think that the way men feel lonely is different from how women feel lonely? If so, how?
4. Personal isolation leads to personal desolation. Have you seen this in a man—someone who had a secret that eventually exploded into high consequences? How did this serve as a warning for you?
5. What hesitations or fears do you have about reaching out to a friend or acquaintance for a deeper relationship?

2
Gritty Initiative

I have been a fitness freak for most of my adult life. My favorite fitness thing to do is mountain biking—the sport I enjoyed with my friend Jon. I have ridden regularly for more than twenty-five years. I even competed in team endurance races, racing my mountain bike on trails in twenty-four-hour races. This sounds crazy, and it was.

When I would stand in an event tent shivering from low overnight temperatures, waiting for my teammate to come in at 2:00 a.m., I would shake my head in disbelief. "Why am I doing this?" I would repeat that until I got the baton from my teammate and headed out on my bike—and then I would remember why!

Plus, we got better each year and started placing within the top three in many of the races, eventually getting first place in a pretty competitive race after ten tries. That really made standing and shivering in an event tent at 2:00 a.m. worth it!

When I was about to turn fifty years old, I wanted to change it up a bit, so I started training for triathlons. As a complement to the training, my wife and I joined a CrossFit/circuit training gym. It was something we could do together, and it was good strength training for triathlons. We worked out together several times a week.

Because the gym was small and used a group workout format, the same people tended to come to the same time slots. A sense of community developed. It was mostly limited to the time we all spent together waiting for class to begin, talking smack to each other about when our workouts were stronger than the other person's, or commenting on the difficulty level of the workout while we all wiped our sweaty faces as we were leaving.

But there was this one guy, Travis, who started coming after we had been there for a while. He stood out to me. In part, he had a military physique—broad shoulders and muscular legs. But he also had a core that was bulky from too many calories and not enough workouts. I could relate. He also kept to himself and didn't interact much with people. He wasn't unfriendly, just not very social.

When I see someone circling on the outside, socially, I always try to bring them into the inside—I have done that since I was a kid. So I started to initiate small conversations with Travis, commenting on the workouts. We were similarly matched and we had a friendly but unspoken competition going on.

I wanted to get to know him a little more, so I finally asked him about a tattoo on his leg. It was a military-style tattoo that touted loyalty and never forgetting.

"Cool tattoo," I said as I motioned my head toward his tattoo.

"Thank you. I served in Afghanistan for two tours. I lost some good friends over there." I could tell his loss was profound.

"I appreciate that you served, and I am really sorry your friends had to die while they were serving. I have never served, and I have never been in a vocation where I feared for my life. I don't think guys like me have a clue what serving is really like. I really do mean it when I say thanks for serving. I really feel blessed by guys like you."

He nodded in appreciation.

"That's why I am here—working out. I got a pretty gnarly injury on my last tour. My knees and my back are pretty trashed because of it. I have had a ton of rehab, and this is the next step. Got to get my tone back and my stomach shrunk."

I suddenly felt less fit, since I was not working through any injuries other than muscle soreness and MAMOS (middle-aged man onset stiffness—my own made-up medical syndrome.) For him to be there working out, and especially running on the treadmill, competing with me after recovering from his injuries, was a great and inspiring story. I loved it and was humbled by his recovery and his physical and mental toughness.

After that, we were kind of like partners—working out next to each other and calling each other by first name.

I determined in my head that I wanted to be his friend and I wanted to hear more of his story—the story not just of his military service, but of his life. I was waiting for the right opportunity to see if he wanted to grab coffee and lunch. But I didn't want him to think I was weird or that I was some sort of creeper. So I kept putting it off.

One day he said, "Isn't Naylor your last name?"

"Yep, that's my last name."

Then I started my own conversation. "Wait... What...? How did he know my last name?"

So I asked him.

"How did you know my last name?"

"I just figured it out."

I remembered he had some military police experience, so he probably stalked me—just a little bit.

Here I was, slowly working up the nerve to ask him to have lunch with me. And it looked like maybe he was interested in getting to know me better too. My asking him questions about his tattoo didn't freak him out. Him figuring out my last name didn't freak me out. We had some mutual interest in getting to know each other some more.

During this time, I was doing some preliminary writing for this book. I joined a writer's group for input and camaraderie. I was sharing some of this writing with the group. One of my retired friends, Cyn (short for Cynthia), chimed in, "It's like you guys are wanting to date each other."

I laughed. "We are, but not at all for romantic reasons. I think we want to be friends."

But we didn't get to be anything but gym partners. He suddenly stopped coming to the workouts.

I know what you are thinking—that it was because of our conversations. He did think I was a creeper.

I am certain it was not for that reason. After all, he was more of the creeper than I was, since he figured out my last name. I think he got a different job—he had been looking for one. I was pretty disappointed—both in the loss of a potential friendship and in my lack of initiative beyond the casual workout conversation. I missed it.

What did I learn from this friendship that barely had a beginning?

Sometimes being drawn to each other as friends never goes anywhere because both potential friends are waiting for the other to go first. And then if they do go first, they keep it too shallow.

We'll be getting to a total of eight ways to add value to male friendships. The first is taking the initiative. Somebody's got to go first and try to get a friendship started. See if the potential is there.

It's simple enough in theory. Hard, evidently, in practice.

TAKING THE INITIATIVE—IT'S IN OUR DNA

I recently preached a sermon about knowing the good but not doing the good. For some reason, our human nature has the uncanny ability to know things that are more perception than knowledge. We just know some things before we really come to know them. Perception, by its nature, is ambiguous and undemanding—really opening up options for us to further explore and act on. When it comes to relationships, our perception can work both ways— keeping us out of bad relationships and keeping us out of good ones. The reason it keeps us out of good relationships is because of the subtleties of perception. We treat them more as suggestions. We can take it or leave it.

For male friendships, too much of the time men leave it, rather than jumping in and taking the initiative for deep, meaningful, gritty friendships. We perceive that a guy we meet could be a good friend. But we don't move on it. We perceive that we are wallowing in shallow relationships, but we don't move on it. We perceive our buddy is struggling and may even be lonely or depressed. But we don't move on it. Why would men let something so important slip away?

WHAT MEN STRIVE FOR FIRST

When asked, most men would agree that it is easier for women to have deeper and meaningful relationships with other women. Statistically, this is true, even though many women feel really lonely too.

Most men would likely agree that women are especially equipped to establish and maintain relationships with other women. This, though, is not true. Women have no corner on the psychological market for starting up and maintaining friendships. In reality, things like empathy, compassion, and love aren't really more prevalent in women than in men. Those are characteristics that make us distinctly human, regardless of gender.

According to Dr. Todd B. Kashdan, a psychologist and professor of psychology at George Mason University, the big difference between men and women and how they initiate relationships comes down to motivation—or the things that motivated us or what we strive after. For men, our main striving is not relationships.

Personal strivings are the central projects that people think about, plan for, and allocate time and energy toward. Strivings provide information about what a person wants as well as the type of person they wish to be. Men disproportionally strive for wealth, success, and power compared to women. Women tend to have a different instruction manual for life, putting a premium on nurturing and befriending other people. This doesn't mean that the average woman is unconcerned about success and status, but that this is less likely to be done without checking in on friendships to ensure they attain their highest potential.[16]

One of Kashdan's colleagues, clinical psychologist Thomas Joiner, after years of research, says,

> Men appear to enjoy many advantages in society—on average they make more money, have more power, and enjoy a greater degree of social freedom than women. But many men pay a high price for the pursuit

---

[16] Todd B. Kashdan, "Why Do Men Have a Hard Time Making Friends?" Psychology Today, October 24, 2011, https://www.psychologytoday.com/us/blog/curious/201110/why-do-men- have-hard-time-making-friends.

of success and power. Taking family and friends for granted, men will often let relationships take a back seat to their professional ambitions, only to ultimately find themselves with few real friends they can rely on in hard times.

So men are strivers. They are motivated to strive, even created to strive. By the time men give their main attention to their masculine motivations and strivings of power, success, and money, and then to their families, there is little left over for the "luxury" of friendships. This is detrimental to the masculine soul, leaving it emotionally, spiritually, and even physically impoverished. This is a dangerous cocktail of neglect, apathy, distraction, and laziness.

And it turns out, this is not how men were designed. Men are not just the initiators of power and passion; they are also the initiators of relationships - gritty ones!

THE FIRST WAY TO ADD RELATIONAL

VALUE IS BY TAKING THE INITIATIVE

Sometimes when you take a look at classic books that have stood the test of time and life application, it is pretty amazing what's in them. That is how the Bible is for me. Sometimes when I dive into the deeper parts of the Bible, I get blown away by the relevancy, especially for masculinity.

One of the most profound verses for me is in the first chapter of Genesis. As the creation story is being told, there is a verse that can really change things for men and women, for marriage, for families, and even for friendships: "God created man in his own image, in the image of God he created him; male and female he created them" (Genesis 1:27, English Standard Version).

In the beginning of the verse, the word for man is more of a generic term that can be likened to humankind. God created humans and they were created to bear the image of God— to reflect aspects of God in human form and experience. The generic reference is clarified in the last phrase. Humankind is described as male and female. These words have a lot of dimension and depth to them. They far exceed physical, moral, and social attributes. They reach deeper into the DNA of masculinity and femininity.

I have paraphrased the meaning of these two important words. The word for male is "the remembering one." The word for female is "the surrounding one."[17] The male is the one who remembers things—important, life-giving things. This communicates vision, passion, and focus.

As you continue in the creation story, you see that Adam, the first man, was given instructions for living from God himself and he was left to it. In those instructions he was given some guidelines to stay within, namely not to eat of the fruit of a certain tree. Fruit from a tree—really? Even that is a wonderfully interesting discussion, but it reaches beyond our quest to understand masculinity and friendship.

Adam commences the work of living, managing the garden, harvesting fruit, and naming the animals. During that work, Adam notices that the animals all have another animal of their kind. For Adam, though, no match was present.

In God's great compassion and provision, he created Eve— the surrounding one. Eve joins Adam in the commencing of

---

17 The Hebrew word for male is "the one who remembers God." The word for female is "to pierce" or "the one who is pierced."

human living while maintaining a vibrant and personal relationship with God, each other, and their surroundings.

This is a man's book. So forgive me if this is a little too graphic for you. But let's back up a moment and think about the meaning behind the word "male" and what happened that day in the garden, and has continued to happen every day since.

Let's start with the physical attributes of the remembering one, the one who remembers vision and stands up—erect—to provide purpose and passion for living. Are you getting what I am tiptoeing around? Well, stay with me. What about the surrounding one and the physical attributes associated with that? Okay, so I am talking about sex here. As the man "stands firm and erect," the woman surrounds him. The man offers his masculine self to the female who surrounds him, and great sex ensues.

Outside of the sexual realm, it is the same. The man offers vision, passion, and direction to the female, and she surrounds it and nurtures it. It is a great design of teamwork and relationship.

That is the design for marriage. It is also the design for relationships. Of course, we have left the sexual realm now! But what the psychologist said earlier in this chapter about men is actually biblical and practical and perpetuating. Men are supposed to be initiators of vision, passion, and relationship!

Fast-forward to Chapter Three of Genesis. Eve is living the garden life, and confusion enters into paradise. She is tempted by a serpent (the devil), who provokes her to doubt God's goodness. She takes the forbidden fruit, snatches a bite while offering a bite to her husband— who was there with her (Genesis 3:6). Many scholars agree that the presence of Adam was more than him walking up on Eve as she wiped the fruity juice off her face. He was present when she was being tempted to question the vision that Adam had passed on to her. There is

Gritty Friendships | 27

no record that God passed vision to Eve. He passed it to Adam, who passed it to Eve. We know she had caught (surrounded) the vision, because when she was being cast into doubting God, she restated the instructions God had given Adam. (She did add one thing, probably just for the sake of drama.) But the enlarged travesty of the situation is that Adam, the one who was supposed to stand firm and erect by remembering vision, didn't. He abstained from taking the initiative in the situation, remained silent and passive. He compromised living for him, his wife, and his offspring.

When it comes to masculine relationships, men do the same thing. We perceive of a potential friendship...and we remain passive. We wait for the other guy to go first. We perceive that we could have a close friendship, but we wait to see if the other guy goes first. We perceive a buddy could use a companion to work through hard things in his life, but we wait until he asks—until he goes first. That is a tragic masculine abdication, and it goes against the design for the one who was not only created first but was asked to make the moves first.

A FORMULA FOR GRITTY INITIATIVE

When I think about my potential but failed relationship with Travis at my circuit training gym, I wanted to do better. I got a second chance. And I did some things a little differently.

Shortly after Travis disappeared, a guy started attending my church. Just like Travis, he stood out to me. He was young and full of energy. He seemed determined and focused. I heard he was an Ironman triathlete. So I applied my short formula for taking the initiative.

We started to meet weekly and became close friends—one of my closest. But the short formula for the start of our relationship was the same: grabbing onto a common interest, asking answerable questions, being genuinely interested in his story, following up, and repeating.

Grab onto a common interest

This first step shouldn't be that difficult for men. It's a natural way of thinking for us, since we are strivers. A part of striving is doing reconnaissance for commonalities—things that look and feel familiar to us and things that make us feel comfortable, and things that are fun for us. This step takes our perceptions one step further. Knowing what we have in common allows us to predict how to act. It allows things to pass through our grid. We usually quickly learn about commonalities or differences. We decide how much we like people. We quickly ascertain how much more of an investment we want to make. We do all these things in moments. Even though it is a little egocentric at the onset, we always are looking for common things in people we encounter. We look for people who look like us, act like us, think like us, play like us.

Once we determine that, it is easy to carry on a conversation. I can't tell you how many fun conversations I have had simply because I notice an Ironman tattoo on a guy's calf (I know—there is that creepy tattoo thing again). And that is with strangers. Taking the initiative with a friend should be even easier, because common interests are what brought you together as friends in the first place.

Even for me this is easy, and really I don't have a lot in common with a lot of guys. I am mechanically challenged (mechanically disinterested is a better description). I don't enjoy sports unless it is mountain biking or triathlon. When people start talking about football, I glaze over for lack of information and interest. For years I never even got invited to Super Bowl parties. I just reeked of non-sports. But the common interests we should really look for are things more important than football or triathlons anyway.

All men struggle with common things like how to be a quality husband or an impacting dad. How is my job part of the long-term picture for my family, for my wife, for me? How does all this fit into my spiritual life and my spiritual development? Am I stagnant or am I growing? Those are always common interests men have—always! So ask them about that...which takes us to the next easy step.

Ask answerable questions

I recently had lunch with a friend I don't see very often. I was excited to see him, but I left not really feeling connected to him or fulfilled by having spent time with him. I think he might have felt differently.

While we ate (or really, while I ate), I asked a lot of questions. He shared a lot of stories and information. My plate was empty. His was filled—both actually and proverbially. Granted, I encouraged all of this because I kept asking questions that he could answer. I asked about his family. I asked about his hobbies. I asked some spiritual questions, since we both love Jesus. I asked about a couple of his hobbies and trips he had taken recently to indulge them. Some of the questions were light. Some of them were probing.

Soon we ran out of time and went our separate ways. As I drove away, I had a nagging feeling about not feeling connected to him. It was because we didn't make time to have the conversation be two-sided. It was not reciprocated. He didn't have the opportunity to ask me any questions. I didn't feel super connected to him, but I think he felt pretty connected to me, not because I am all that and a bag of chips, but because he got to share some of his current story with me. I would have enjoyed telling him a bit about my upcoming triathlons and some things happening in my church, or maybe even some personal things like some of the things I am working on in my emotional life.

Asking answerable questions really isn't that hard. Just fish for something you have in common, the things that drew you together in the first place, and ask some questions about it. And be careful not to present a question gauntlet for them to walk through...which leads us to the next step.

Be genuinely interested in their story

Here is another quick story about a time when I learned something important about asking questions. It was with a relative who I was close to when I was growing up. As we became adults, we drifted apart, geographically and relationally. He came to visit after a few years of not seeing each other. As we were catching up, and while I was practicing the second step (ask answerable questions), I noticed there was some tension mounting. He was seeming to be a little defensive as I asked him questions. I was genuinely interested in his story—like all of it. But he felt inspected by me. He felt like he was walking through a gauntlet of life questions, because I was moving through them too quickly. He felt more inspected than supported, and I seemed like more of an evaluator than a friend.

People's stories are fascinating—they really are. Being genuinely interested in their story is not so you can make commentary on it; it is so you can relate to their story and therefore actually become a part of their story. I am continually surprised by how quickly men will open up to other men when you ask a question and listen and follow-up with questions about the story they are telling you.

And be interested for their sake, not for yours. Don't just ask questions to learn tips on how to be a better parent, entrepreneur, or whatever. Those things will be the icing on the cake. And be sure to let them know how much you gleaned from hearing their story!

Follow up

Have you ever heard of sharer's remorse? It's when you share something with someone and afterward wished you hadn't. Most of the time this remorse is only on the sharer's side. They think they might have shared too much, been too weak, insecure, or emotional. This is especially true for men because they aren't accustomed to sharing some of the deeper things of life. One way to minimize sharer's remorse is to do a quick follow-up to a meaningful conversation.

This just happened on the day I am writing this. After my run, I went into the sauna. Part of the sauna man code is that you don't make too much eye contact with sweaty men with very few clothes on. As I came in, I saw there were two guys in there, scoped out the appropriate distance to maintain, and sat down. I was getting into my little sauna time, thinking about my day while I watched the shapes my sweat drops were making as they hit the wood floor (don't you do that too?). Then I heard someone say my name. It was a friend I hadn't seen in over a year. We used to get together regularly. But he drifted away, and I didn't pursue him when he did.

We had a great talk. I practiced the methods I have described here. I asked a few answerable questions. He did too. I told him about the Ironman I had just finished, and he told me about the struggles he had about turning fifty, which was that very day. I loved the interaction. It was a good time of connecting.

And I just texted him, telling him how much I enjoyed seeing him and catching up a bit today. I'm hoping we can rekindle our relationship! Live update: He just texted back. I think we might have some coffee soon.

Repeat

After these steps are done, you're not done. You have to keep taking the initiative to keep the friend-fire warm! So keep it going. Set up a time for lunch or coffee. You'd be surprised how often men say yes to an invitation like this. I have been doing this for years and have only been turned down a few times. It is super easy to get sucked back into the strivings (career, family) I talked about in this chapter and neglect important and meaningful friendships that you could make gritty. But taking the initiative for relationships is part of the man DNA. And men are just way better men when they make male friendships a priority!

A SECOND CHANCE

All of these steps require someone—you—to take the initiative, adding friendships to your list of important strivings, and being vulnerable and risking a little rejection along the way. Remember Travis, the circuit training guy I thought would become my friend? I still wonder about that—about him. With Travis, I only got to number three.

But soon after that, I got a second chance to do better with my new friend from church who I mentioned earlier.

With him, I didn't stall out on number three, but tenaciously kept moving forward. I asked him about how our friendship developed, so I could use it in this book. He agreed to have a chat about it. I am including it here so you can see a model of how I proceeded through the steps I share in this chapter.

I made some good coffee, one of the things we both have a deep appreciation for. We met up in my backyard as the sun was coming up. After some catching up on life and family, I asked him what he remembered about when we first met.

"Well, you were one of the pastors of the church I had just started attending. I wanted to get involved in serving somewhere, so I reached out to the worship pastor about helping with the sound/audio system, because I had done that before. I came early one day to begin to get trained on the sound system. I didn't know if I should just walk into the rehearsal, so I was meandering around in the lobby. You approached me to say hi and to see if I needed help."

"I do remember that," I replied. "I had noticed you before that, but I hadn't gotten to meet you yet. I saw that you were fit, and I wondered what you did to stay in shape. And you had some cool tattoos." (I know this seems like a creepy trend for me.)

Someone told me he was an Ironman, which wasn't true yet. As it turns out, he had just started training to compete in his first Ironman. After I heard that, I reached out to him on social media, asking if we could get together about triathloning, since I had an interest in doing an Ironman too.

And so our relationship began. He was the instrumental guy who finally got me to commit to doing an Ironman. And my wife has still not forgiven him. Just kidding. She knows I am a better, well-rounded man when I train for a goal like an Ironman. But he did talk me into it.

Soon after that, we met up for master swim class. I was pretty intimidated, but showing up with someone who had been there before helped a lot. He kept pushing me more and more into triathlon and I soon bought a triathlon bike—which I love! We started riding, swimming, and running together when we could.

It seems like we moved on from Ironman talks quickly, though. I asked him how that happened.

"Well, to be honest, I was looking for some connection, especially with a man who was older than me."

I almost spit out some of the great coffee. "Thanks for that reminder. I was actually a little bummed when I realized I was only a couple of years younger than your dad."

"Sorry about that—but you're a young guy for your age. But that was actually an important part of your friendship, then and now. I was pretty excited that you reached out to me. I saw that—at the risk of offending your aging ego yet again—you had 'experience' in relationships and life since you were older than me. But I was a little intimidated to ask anyone to be that kind of friend. The kind of friend that talked about deep and meaningful things. Things I was wondering about but afraid to bring up in other relationships. Things like masculinity, career, ego, marriage, kids, God, the Bible, insecurities, psychological stuff, struggles with my adult parents."

"That's a big list. When I reached out to you, I had no idea you were that screwed up. I just wanted to find out about triathlons. Just kidding. I have all of those same struggles too, except the kids part. But I have a bunch of adult kids in the church—like you!"

"I know, all of us guys have the same list. But the thing I was excited about was that you were the one who took the initiative. You were outgoing. You knew stuff. You shared stuff. You were real, authentic, and vulnerable. You quickly became like

Gritty Friendships | 35

a sensei to me because you knew what you were doing in life and in relationships."

I cringed a little. "Well, thanks for that yet again. How many times will you be reminding me of my age in this conversation? And thanks for thinking I had my stuff together. The truth is, we both share our stuff. Even though we have an age gap, we don't really have an issue gap. We are usually wrestling with very similar things."

I refilled our coffee and greeted my dogs, which my wife had let out into the yard by then. It didn't feel like we were done yet. He kept going - getting grittier by the moment.

"Well, this sounds pathetic and man-creepy, but I was in the market for male friendship. I had a little bit of social anxiety and had moved into a season of introvertedness. I didn't think I was in a position to be an initiator. I didn't think I had enough maturity to offer anything to my peers. I had tried to reach out and had been let down. The men I approached were inconsistent and nominally interested in real stuff. I didn't experience any depth to the relationships. I was disappointed and I was tired of being rejected. I figured my desire for depth must be abnormal, because no one else seemed to want depth. It seemed like that's not what men do. I have learned since that men's priorities are work, family, repeat. And until they hit a crisis or something, they don't make male friendships a priority."

I totally agreed with him. I had literally hundreds of situations that proved it true. That seemed like a good stopping spot, so we converted to more important topics like mountain biking and triathlons, made some lame jokes, and said goodbye until our next chat the next week. The talk couldn't have gone better for me and for this book. It was exactly what I hoped for. I wanted to see if he had experienced the formula I like to use for initiating relationships. He had!

So here is the formula again:

- Grab onto a common interest.
- Ask answerable questions.
- Be genuinely interested in their story.
- Follow up.
- Repeat.

BE A RELATIONSHIP INITIATOR

I have thought back to some of the other closer relationships that I have now. I used the same formula, and I plodded along and didn't stall out. For years I have been intentional about taking the initiative in male friendships. I have sought out relationships with men, especially those who seemed they might be isolated. And almost never have I been turned down. In fact, never have I been turned down. When I have taken the initiative, my relationships always deepened.

In thirty years of making male friendships a priority, only three times have men, when I asked them if they wanted to get together on a regular basis, declined. And the reason they declined was because of their hectic schedule and one guy thought I was too busy to make time for him—and that was an entirely different issue to address...

My closing point is this. Men want to connect with men. Men are designed to be connectors and initiators. When we don't, we are lesser men. So stop being lesser. Be greater, and take some other men with you. Get gritty.

DISCUSSION QUESTIONS

1. Think about a close friendship you have or had at one point. How did it get started? Who took the initiative first?
2. When a male friend reached out to you to do something fun, to drink some coffee, to go see an action movie (basically, when he took the initiative with you), how did you respond? How did it make you feel?
3. What things keep you from initiating a conversation with a stranger or someone you don't really know that well?
4. What keeps you from initiating a deeper relationship with one or two of your male friends?

3
Gritty Experiences

I had never been in a rehab commencement before. I have been a part of hundreds and hundreds of reconciliation meetings as a pastor and life coach. This one was different. I was sitting in a big circle of strangers - except for one - my brother. Actually he was pretty much a stranger since we had not seen each other for many, many years. His daughter was also in the circle. She was in her early twenties. The last time I saw her, she hadn't even started kindergarten.

The reasons for our extended estrangement were as simple as they were complicated. At first it was geographic distance, then it was idealistic differences intensified by family drama. Eventually, there was a misunderstanding that made the rift seem too large to cross for either of us. Even though I had gotten used to it, there were times when I would think of him and I would tense my lips and shake my head from side to side in disbelief. We were so close growing up. I would have never thought that we would not be a part of each other's lives. And I am a relationship expert...

He was the one who crossed the rift first. He was going into a residential rehabilitation program the next day. He would be there for a couple of months to finally deal with his alcoholism that had brought him really close to death. We spoke for more than two hours. We cleared up some misunderstandings, reviewed some childhood traumas that had plagued both of us and eagerly entered back into a fun-loving relationship. It was as natural as it was unbelievable. We began to talk weekly after that - still do!

Six weeks went by quickly for me, and intensely for him. He called me to let me know he was about to complete his rehabilitation and was about to move into a long-term housing situation that would help keep him sober as he transitioned back into his career and life. When he told me the date of his commencement, I stirred inside. I was going to be there. I had missed his high school graduation - I was not going to miss this graduation. I knew this was a unique opportunity with great relational magnitude and I wasn't about to let it pass. It was an opportunity to create a meaningful experience. So I booked a rental car and took off for Denver, Colorado - a 14 hour drive. I reached out to my foster sister whom I hadn't seen in 40 years and we set up a time to get together - which ended up being really meaningful too. I reached out to my best friend from 6th grade through high school graduation and set up some time with him too - which is always meaningful.

I was there to see my brother cross an important life-bridge to sobriety! And it was great. It was one of the more meaningful experiences I have had in my life - and not just because the administrator of the program told me I looked like Rob Lowe in front of everyone. I graciously (and enthusiastically - on the inside) accepted the compliment! It was really meaningful for him too - my being there - and not just because I looked like Rob Lowe. His accomplishment of sobriety was momentous. Being back together as brothers and friends was too!

Months after the trip to his commencement was over, we were chatting about my visit. I asked him what stood out about me being there. His first comment was that I showed up in a Camaro. He said it was like a movie. In full candor, I rented a Camaro because the reservation got messed up and it was the only thing left - what was I to do!?! Between his program administrator saying I looked like Rob Lowe and driving a Camaro, I think he was a little proud.

But there was more to it for sure. He told me that he wanted to ask me to come, but was afraid to - he didn't want to be presumptuous. He didn't know what my life demands were at the time - after all our lives had been separated for 16 years. After showing up and making a little scene with my good looks (as if...) and a cool car (definitely true!!!), it came time for the commencement.

Like I said, I had never been at one before. They all sat in a big circle so he could see all of their faces. And one by one, they affirmed his growth and his future. It really was phenomenal! When it was my turn, I first let them know that I knew him the longest than anyone there - so there's that! After that, I told my brother that what everyone saw in him had always been there but had just gone to sleep because of alcohol. I was excited to see him awake again! And then he had me pray the blessing on him. It was an honor both of us will remember.

In my story I just shared, I hope you can see a few things that I did to create a meaningful moment for us - one that ended up changing our relationship. Here are some things to remember.

Creating meaning isn't as hard as it sounds

I am a big change-proponent. But the change I advocate for is recalibrated change. What I mean is that sustainable change has to be slow and incremental. The problem with that kind of change is that most people are already maxed out. All of their connections - especially for relationships - are already taken. All of the schedule is scheduled. All their learning is tapped out. Be this as it may - or may not -[18] the most impacting change is made from tapping into habits, thinking, and demands that already exist in your life. The magic sauce is to make small tweaks by adding some things to things that already exist in your life - preferences, habits, hobbies, inclinations (healthy and legal ones) and passions. It is the same for gritty friendships with men - we just have to tap into some stuff that's already there and make it more and better.

For instance, from my story above, my brother's rehab commencement was not in any way orchestrated, negotiated or carried off by me. The wheels were already in motion when he told me about it. When he told me about it, it was a few days away. This event was hopefully only going to happen once. It was important to him. Our relationship was once again important to me. I wanted it to be gritty again. So I tapped into it instead of tapping out of it. Too often, we tap out of gritty opportunities instead of tapping into them.

Here are five ways you can tap into stuff already a part of you, your life and your relationships and you can create grit and meaning along the way.

---

[18] Actually, this is not very true for most humans. We have an incredible capacity for ongoing learning -more than any other creature. We have more capacity than we even begin to tap into. But that starts to reach beyond this book and back to my first book about emotional intelligence and neurogenesis. See Emotalerting - The Art of Managing the Moment.

Creating gritty, meaningful moments is really about paying attention to opportunities and capturing momentum that already is moving

Once in a while creating something new can be fun too. But be careful not to create an experience that doesn't connect with your friend. I remember a friend of mine a few years back invited me to a spring training baseball game. I was happy that he was making a move toward me by inviting me - we had never done anything together outside of our small group in our church. I was having a stressful week. You would think that a break from the stress would be good - and it was. As soon as I sat down, I engaged my stress in my head instead of the relationship with my friend. This was really easy because I have little to no interest in baseball or most organized sports. Apparently between my stress and my disinterest, I looked really bored. My friend later apologized for selecting baseball as an outing for us. I felt a little bad about that, but the fact was it was the wrong experience for me. There was no momentum that was already moving.

Capturing momentum that is already moving does require paying a little attention to passing comments or common interests. I recently started a new friendship with a triathlon guy - a specimen of man who turned 60 this year, but looks ½ his age - well, at least ¾ his age. He has a reputation that precedes him. I became aware of him through social media. He has a pretty large following. At one triathlon, he sang the national anthem. He could sing too! We were in the same age category (he has since aged up into the next one - less competition for me). Before the swim started, our age group was in the water treading while we waited for the start. I ended up next to him and called him out by his social media name and thanked him for singing. He said thank you, the race started and I never saw him again - like I said, his reputation precedes him and so does his pace in triathlons.

A couple of years later, we ended up becoming members at the same new gym. Our swim schedule started to sync up and we started chatting. We ended up grabbing an after workout snack one day and found out we had a lot more in common than triathlons. We shared a common faith and were dedicated to Jesus and to the local church. We seemed to click even more.

A few weeks ago, we were talking about upcoming triathlon events we were training for. He is going to compete in an event in a location I have competed at before. I told him maybe I would drive up and cheer him on. He was excited to hear that and mentioned that his family wasn't going to be able to make it, and maybe we could drive up together. It is still a few months away, and there are logistics to work out, but I am hoping it comes together. I don't know how good of friends we might become or not, but I like talking with him and hanging out with him. When we were doing both, he mentioned something in addition to triathlon - his faith - that I tapped into that may give us an opportunity to create a meaningful experience.

When connecting with others, it's important to accept them where they are, not where you believe they should be.

You are somewhere on your journey and your friends are somewhere on theirs, which means you will both be at different stages in your journeys. If you compare your path with another's, you can miss out on the opportunity to make a meaningful connection while you are both in the same place - whether it is a moment or a season. And if your mission is to get them to a point you think they should be at, they will probably sense it. And many of us men do not really appreciate being someone's project - especially if we didn't ask them to change us in the first place.

I had a conversation with a friend recently about a relationship he has with a friend. They have been struggling with connecting for a few years. In the course of another conversation about the struggle and his desire to to be closer than they were, another friend offered a potential reason for the drift. It was like a light bulb for my friend. He was sure that was the cause of their lack of closeness and even frustration in their relationship. He reached out to his friend and shared his discovery of the source of their relationship problem. He was sure that if they could agree on that, then they could get through the relationship struggle. It was not a light bulb moment for his friend. Instead of a light bulb of discovery, it was like a wad of Christmas lights that was better tossed in the garbage than detangled. It didn't make sense to him and he didn't think that was the problem at all. And it sounded like he felt "shoulded on". "You should agree with me about this." When we feel like someone just "shoulded" on us, well, it usually stinks.

When we connect with each other to make gritty moments, you should (yes I am shoulding on you right now) be more selfless than selfish. What I mean is that you should remember whether you are trying to create a gritty moment for them or for you. If you are intentionally creating the gritty moment, then it really is more about them than it is about you. It will become gritty for you when it becomes meaningful for them. So you have to do something meaningful to them first and you will get your meaning second.

Seek Adventure

Mindless activities are - well, mindless. I am talking about something like mountain biking, one of my choices, is really interactive - with nature. Negotiating the path engages the brain. I do a lot of triathlon training. So I run on the street a lot. Running on the street could do the same thing, but not as much. The road is way more tame than the trail! Although, it is outdoors. I think a key element in creating meaningful experiences is to do something outdoors - in the open air, with air of excitement.

I have a theory I haven't spent a lot of time researching or developing, so I hesitate to share it with you, but I'll do it anyway. I think the Industrial Revolution ruined men by bringing them indoors from the outdoors and dousing their creativity and innate masculine artistry with mundane factory work. It took labor and artisan crafts that required the work of a man's mind and their hands and transferred them to assembly lines where they were more like machines who were working with machines.[19]

And it morphed in our modern day from the factory to the office and then from the office to the home office and from the home office to virtual living that creates life and adventures that are barely real and certainly safe. Virtual adventures aren't adventures and certainly not gritty because you aren't really getting hurt if you mess up or fail a little bit. The only risk is that you have to go backwards a few levels in your game-world. When you get hurt or die, you just restart the game. I am not saying that pain or death are a requisite for meaningful, gritty experiences, but there is something about adventure that stimulates men's souls and binds them together. Some of my greatest and favorite memories were made during an adventure with a friend or groups of friends.

---

[19] Industrialization, Labor, and Life. Industrialization ushered much of the world into the modern era, revamping patterns of human settlement, labor, and family life. https://education.nationalgeographic.org/resource/industrialization-labor-and-life/

*Adventure, with all its requisite danger
and wildness, is a deeply spiritual
longing written into the soul of man.*

- John Eldredge

One of my go-to books for men is *Wild At Heart* by John Eldredge (Thomas Nelson, 2001). In this book, he contends that men are better and bigger men, or what I would call "gritty", when they commit to a battle, an adventure, and a beauty. These are their God-given drives in the heart of every man. It is very compelling - so much so that I still tell men this is a must read even though it was first released in 2001. For me there are not very many things as compelling as seeing men contend with what Eldridge wrote with tears running down their faces in front of other men in a bagel shop. All three of his contentions are solid in my opinion. And I have more than an opinion. I have seen countless men who get changed by intentionally stepping into what God intended for them in the first place by using this model.

Stepping into a gritty adventure is really manly. There are a lot of ladies who love adventure too. But when men step into an adventure, it ignites some soulful stuff. Just this last weekend, I had a triathlon called The IceMan where we started off by swimming in a freshwater lake in February. It was in Arizona, but the water temperature was 52'. In the dark of the morning before I left, while my wife was still snuggling in the warmth of the bed, I asked her to say a prayer for me. In her prayer, she said, "I don't totally understand this adventure seeking-side of him that would get him out of bed for this today, but bless his effort and keep him safe." She really does understand it since it is a way of life for me - one adventure after the other. I honestly think men are better men - emotionally, physically, intellectually and spiritually - when they include gritty adventures as a part of their life.

Believe it or not, while I am writing this section of this book, I am on a "writing retreat" in Idaho where some of my family lives. It just so happens that my 24 year old nephew was passing through. We literally had 20 minutes to chat because he was on his way out of town. I asked him about the mountain bikes he had in the back of his truck. He told me a quick story of why he had a new mountain bike. He was mountain biking with his friends a year ago, and he slid out next to a cliff. He stopped short from plummeting 200 feet down a cliff, but his bike didn't. I told him I had just written about the adventure side of life and how important it was to men in their own lives and especially in the lives of their relationships. He perked up and agreed with me. He said something like "Lame adventures equal a lame life." He said life gradually gets that way if you stop having good adventures. Words of wisdom from a twenty-something. And he is qualified. He is a young entrepreneur making a great living while maintaining a good balance of adventure and work. Don't let the adventure side of your life die out! Keep it fresh and adventurous so you stay that way too - and do it with your friends.

Create "Windshield Time"

I have some crazy friends who do crazy things - things that ignite their souls as well as their bodies. The soul part feeds their lives. The body part... it breaks their body down, but only for a few days. Some of those friends say the very same things about me. It's a healthy and sick interdependence of being gritty by doing gritty things.

There was one weekend I was competing in the 70.3 mile Ironman in Saint George, Utah - the same place I hope to travel to with my new triathlon friend I already mentioned. It was hard. I had a few physical and mechanical challenges along the way. The 1.1 mile cold water swim started rough for me because I panicked and started breathing erratically (which makes it really hard to swim) and I had to stop on a buoy for 60 seconds to calm my breathing down. I lost my gears before I was halfway through the 56.1 mile bike ride, just a few miles from all the climbs (I lost about 30 minutes from that mishap). The 13.1 mile run was the hardest run I had ever run in training or at competitions. It had way more hard climbs than I trained for and my time suffered there too. My times always suffer on the run, but that's another story for another time. Despite all of this, it was still such a fabulous day and I loved it! One of the best parts of the day was seeing one of my best friends at different parts of the grueling race. He came with me to cheer me on.

The day after we got back, he started an epic adventure of his own. He ran a 250 mile foot race on the mountain trails of Arizona. He climbed over 40,000 feet in 5 days with about ten hours of sleep. It was amazing. I, along with another friend and his family, got to see him off at the start. And then I got to track him on an app, day and night, to see his progress. To be honest, I was a little obsessed. I got up several times in the middle of the night each night to see where he was. It was a grueling and amazing week for both of us. I got to do a FaceTime with him part way through and I got a little emotional when I saw his face. He looked so worn and determined at the same time. I met up with him in the wee hours of the morning on day four of his adventure. I brought a friend who accompanied him on the last 100 miles. My wife, some other friends, and I were able to be super fans at the finish line, screaming like rabid banshees as he crossed the 257 mile finish line! It was so spectacular! I was honored to get a big sweaty and stinky hug at the finish line as I told him how proud I was of him.

But there are a few other beautiful and gritty moments that stood out for me in our two adventures. On the road trip up to Utah and back, we had some great "Windshield Time".

Windshield Time is when friends take a road trip and stare out the windshield of the car and share some deep and meaningful things with each other. Men tend to find it easier to share deeper things when we don't have constant eye contact. My friend and I got to do that. I learned some things about him that I was previously unaware of - a little deep and a little dark. I understood him more - his personality and his motivations. I think he learned some things about me too. Inevitably, we got closer on that trip. I think the emotion I felt for him when I saw his weariness and determination was catapulted a bit by the closeness I experienced as we looked out the windshield and shared from our hearts a few days earlier.

So, here's my recommendation for you: do some crazy, gritty and meaningful things with your buddies. You don't have to be quite as sick and crazy as we are with Ironman competitions and 250 mile multi-day ultra runs, but you could take a drive to a cool hiking trail or a mountain lake. As you stare out the windshield, see what comes up. Ask about career aspirations or how close they are to their wife or kids. Ask how their parents are doing. My friend and I did not have a checklist. We just took a road trip together and ended up having deep and meaningful conversation, ultimately strengthening our bond.

Allow for Accidental Emotional Detoxing

One reason men are experiencing an isolation epidemic is because they are afraid to let stuff out - to let the toxic bubbles of living pop instead of churning around in our psyche and emotions. And the effects of this churning are real and damaging. We all know that stress does as much to our bodies as it does to our minds and our psyche. Stress does not discriminate. Both men and women suffer many effects of stress: physically, psychologically, and behaviorally. Although there are definitely some outcomes of stress that are exclusive or more frequent for men like prostate cancer, erectile dysfunction, male infertility, cardiovascular disease, chronic gastric problems, chronic pain and frequent colds and infections.[20]

There is a bit of a double-whammy here. Men are way less likely to process their stress with anyone other than themselves. And stress causes them to isolate away from friendships - a triple-whammy[21]. They are already isolating themselves. They don't share their stress. Because they are stressed, they isolate even more. That's three layers of isolation!

Men should (yep, shoulding on you again) learn to process their stress differently. They should stop keeping it to themselves, making themselves sicker and more stressed than they already are.

How should a man emotionally detox? There are retreats for this. But that is definitely not a go-to thing for most men. Let's go away for the weekend and sleep in a bunk house so we can smell each other's gas, hear each other snore and then go to workshops to learn how to feel and express our emotions. Where do I sign up! Not!

---

[20] How to Tell When a Man Is Stressed. https://www.healthline.com/health/stress-symptoms-in-men#complications. Downloaded Mar 1, 2023.
[21] Ibid

I am all about understanding your own, and other's emotions, but if it is too over-orchestrated then men are defensive at the start and offensive at the end. And getting a buddy to sign up and pay for a retreat weekend requires admitting that you need some work. We will get there in this book, but at this stage, we are just trying to connect and make some meaningful memories - kind of like putting some money in the friendship bank. We'll make accountable withdrawals a little later.

Men almost have to be tricked into identifying and sharing their emotions. It is more likely to happen when they are doing other things that are fun and emotionally detoxing. If men are invited into emotional detoxing formally, they are skeptical, evasive and dismissive. But if men find themselves suddenly sharing some stuff from their life that is stressing them out, it is a different thing. And many times, this kind of sharing is not planned, but comes out of an adventure.

THE REAL MEANING OF GRITTY EXPERIENCES

One of the biggest things that makes a gritty experience meaningful is the connection with people. The experiences are ancillary and value-added. As I remember many, many adventures with my friends over the years, the most memorable parts of them were the unplanned moments that were fun and that were also emotionally, accidentally and positively invasive and transformative - and we just wanted to have fun, but we got meaningful experiences as an add-on!

If you were to circle up your friends and ask them for the meaning of life, you would likely get as many answers as there were friends present. As a follower of Jesus, I happen to think there is great meaning in life by serving Jesus and His plan for redeeming people into righteous greatness! Jesus succinctly let us know the meaning of life when he was asked what was most important. His answer: meaningful relationships - with God and with each other (Matthew 22:35-40, Mark 12:28-34, and Luke 10:25-28).

Relationships are key. Relationships are vital. The thing about men is that they are having a little too much relationship with only themselves. And we know too much about ourselves to rely on that relationship to bring ultimate meaning to our life. Can we know real meaning? I think so.

There is a super-important distinction that can make the difference between living a life where you're pining for meaning or living a life full of meaning. If you keep looking for the meaning of life, you will always end up disappointed. But if you check in with yourself about what you've actually experienced as meaningful and treat those experiences as your best education, then meaning becomes a wellspring and a renewable resource. You will never have to hunt for meaning again or pine for meaning again. You will have stepped firmly onto the path of understanding how to make meaning by making meaning.[22]

CREATING GRITTY EXPERIENCES CREATES MEANING

I started this chapter with the story of me creating a meaningful experience for my brother by attending his alcohol rehabilitation commencement. As I drove the really cool Camaro home from Denver to Phoenix, I had myself as company. I did a lot of thinking and processing. When I got home, I was sharing my great experience with my wife. And all of a sudden I started

---

[22] Maisel, Dr Eric. The Good Man Project. September 19, 2020. https://goodmenproject.com/featured-content/what-do-men-find-meaningful-kpkn/. Mar 29, 2022.

bawling as I confessed something to her. It was an ugly belly bawl - really intense. I think she has seen me cry like that only one time - a year before when my dad unexpectedly died. They were similar cries. They were both about loss - one already realized and one I didn't want to realize.

In my pursuit to create a meaningful experience for my brother, I created one for me. As my belly shook and my face contorted in front of my wife, I said, "I forgot how much I loved him. When we thought he was going to die before this, I was almost numb to any loss it would be for me. But now, I remember how much I love him, and I can barely handle the thought of losing him again. I am confident in his healing and in his determination to overcome the alcoholism that almost killed him, but now I am scared. What if he doesn't."

I created a meaningful experience by creating a meaningful and gritty experience. And the effort and the risk of pain and loss was well worth it. As I write this, my brother is more than a year sober. He is integrating back into regular life with deep and meaningful relationships with people he had ostracized and alienated. We talk and laugh deeply every week! Before last year, I thought our relationship was over and as dead as my family and his friends thought he was about to be. I have my brother back. My life has increased meaning.

People are important. As my Deistic friend Jesus Christ iterated, next to a relationship with God, relationships with other people are vital. Through those relationships, we learn to love ourselves at the same time. So spread some love - enlarge your life by enlarging the depth and meaning of your relationships by creating some gritty experiences.

DISCUSSION QUESTIONS

1. What have been some of the most memorable experiences you experienced with male friends? What makes them stand out for you?
2. How much adventure do you have in your life? When you get to take an adventure, what does it do for you?
3. How often do you talk with your male friends about the stressors in your life? Is there a reason you hesitate to do this?
4. Is it normal for a friend to reach out to you to have some fun or take an adventure? Could it become normal because you take the initiative first?
5. What effect are shallow relationships taking on your life? How could meaningful male friendships change things up for you?

4
Gritty Conversations

There is a lot more to a man's life than sports and weather. It's the other things, like family, ego, and jobs, that get men worked up and even where they mess up more often. Men can have gritty relationships by engaging the things in life that matter and the things that a man can do something about.

I was driving through Las Vegas after a fun breakfast with a good high school friend. I was on my way to Boise, Idaho to spend concentrated time on writing - this book in fact. I got a text from someone in my church asking me to call him when I had the chance. As a pastor who loves life coaching as much as I do preaching and studying, I get requests like this one often enough. We had gone to lunch a few times bantering about the state of the world and religion and such. We enjoyed each other's company. This was unusual because he had never asked me to call him before.

I am a little ashamed and embarrassed to tell you what I started thinking. I quickly went to the negative. Oh, great. He is upset about something and they are leaving the church. What in the [insert pastor approved expletives here] happened. I started conjecturing scenarios and practicing rebuffs. That lasted about one minute, then I called him. I usually jump in to conversations like that to hijack my conjecturing that usually goes too far past reality. That was the case - my conjecturing had no reality. He wanted to pick my brain about a friend's situation. His close friend was having a significant, maybe life and death struggle with alcohol - yep that again. He had already stepped up in some really relevant, risky, and gritty ways.

As he told me the story of his friend's predicament, I was slightly mortified and relieved. I was mortified by yet another story of a solitary man struggling poorly through life. I was simultaneously mortified by my jumping to a negative scenario about why he reached out to talk. He wanted a friend's/pastor's advice about what to do next. It had nothing to do with any unhappiness or discontent with our church. He was fighting for the soul and livelihood of one of his best friends.[23]

Why do we do that? Why do we go negative so quickly and easily? Why am I starting this chapter about engaging important issues with this story about going negative? Well, there is this thing we all live with and talk with and process life with called Negativity Bias. The goal of this chapter is to engage gritty topics with each other for positive life impact. But if most of us are engaging conversations from a negative perspective from the start, it may help to understand where we are starting from.

WHAT IS NEGATIVITY BIAS?

Negativity Bias is a basic human tendency that gives more attention to the bad things that happen, making them seem much more important than they really are.

On the onset, this may seem really tainted and dark. There is a lot of happiness and joy and beauty all around us. Why are we

---

[23] Unfortunately, a couple of months after writing this, my friend lost his friend to alcoholism.

more attracted to this dark underbelly of thinking? We do this to try to make sense of the world. It is how we anticipate, calibrate and retaliate to the constantly moving world around us.

- We pay more attention to negative events than positive ones.
- We learn more from negative outcomes and experiences than we do from positive ones.
- We make decisions based on negative information more than positive data.[24]

There are some good outcomes from filtering the world through a negative lens rather than a positive one:

Protection

We constantly and innately evaluate our environment for threats. This happens in the center parts of our brains where emotion and spirituality live. After that first response, we start reasoning with the other parts of our brain. We are basically hard-wired for negativity. Studies show that observed brain activity in infants have shown that we start practicing basic Negativity Bias when we are six months old. Negativity comes way more naturally than thinking positively. Thinking positively is harder work. An expert in Negativity Bias, Dr Rick Hanson describes our brains like Velcro for negativity and as Teflon for positivity.

As the brain evolved, it was critically important to learn from negative experiences – if one survived them! "Once burned, twice shy." So the brain has specialized circuits that register

---

[24] Cherry, Kendra. What is the Negativity Bias, November 14, 2022
Https://www.very well mind.com/negative-bias-4589618.

negative experiences immediately in emotional memory. On the other hand, positive experiences – unless they are very novel or intense – have standard issue memory systems, and these require that something be held in awareness for many seconds in a row to transfer from short-term memory buffers to long-term storage. Since we rarely do this, most positive experiences flow through the brain like water through a sieve, while negative ones are caught every time. Thus my metaphor of Velcro and Teflon – an example of what scientists call the "negativity bias" of the brain.[25]

Fear of Loss

We respond with more vigor when we fear losing something. We are less motivated and energetic when we long to gain something. This is a demotivating oxymoron. Vision incites us. It calls us to action. Right?! But the reality of our realities is that we instinctively react with fight or flight in the moment in our interior, reacting brain. Vision is a product of the frontal cortex, thinking brain. Getting envisioned happens after we know we are safe in the moment. In any moment thereafter, we have calculated risk and have decided to veto the fear of loss or failure for some long-term gain. The bottom line is we are innately motivated by the negative.

Attentiveness

Many studies show that our brains engage at a quicker and higher level during negative experiences than they do at positive

---

[25] Hanson, Rick. Overcoming the Negativity Bias. https://www.rickhanson.net/overcoming-negativity-bias/. Downloaded March 2, 2023.

ones. Additionally, negative news gains more attention because it is dramatic.

This is great news for an attention deficit disorder poster-child like me. I need all the help I can get to keep my attention focused. I am also an empathetic person which really just means I hate to see people in pain. So I am always on guard for myself and for people. It's an honorable and exhausting curse! I also drink from a glass that is always half-full. I love to believe the best in people and hope for the best for them too. This probably sounds confusing, and it is. Let me summarize it this way: Really I am just a drama king. Aren't we all? We all have a flair for the dramatic. We all drink from the half-empty glass first. This keeps us safe and calibrated for action.

Filtering

We instinctively run any news through the grid of our religion, politics, idealism, etc. to keep offending or undermining factors at bay. This doesn't mean that we are automatically oppositional or categorical, just observational.

Decision-Making

Negative Bias helps us make good decisions. In their famous work, Nobel Prize-winning researchers Kahneman and Tversky found that when making decisions, people consistently place greater weight on negative aspects of an event than they do on positive ones.[26]

---

[26] Kahneman D, Tversky A. Choices, values, and frames. American Psychologist. 1984;39(4): 341-350. doi:10.1037/0003-066x.39.4.341

People Perception

We assess people and their motives quickly. Our go-to grid for evaluation starts from a negative filter. Studies have shown that when given both "good" and "bad" adjectives to describe another person's character, participants give greater weight to the bad descriptors when forming a first impression.[27]

And finally, the reason we are even talking about Negative Bias,

Relationships

The Negativity Bias can have a profound effect on your relationships. This bias might initially lead people not only to expect the worst in situations, but in each other. Whether we like it or not, we all speak a common language: negativity. It is our native tongue since infancy. So in relationships, we all start there. But we don't have to stay there. If we do, then we are all just having one pity party after another, circling the drain of pessimism together.

AM I TOO SCREWED UP IN MY HEAD?

Behold, I am making all things new.

- Jesus Christ - Revelation 21:5

---

[27] Hilbig, Benjamin E. Good things don't come easy (to mind): Explaining framing effects in judgments of truth. Experimental Psychology. 2011;59(1):38-46. doi:10.1027/1618-3169/a000124

And not only this, but we also celebrate in our tribulations, knowing that tribulation brings about perseverance; and perseverance, proven character; and proven character, hope; and hope does not disappoint....

- Apostle Paul - Romans 5:3-5

I had a recent conversation that epitomizes what a lack of hope and vision does to a person. It started with this question: "Am I too screwed up in my head?" The question came from a life-long friend. We spent about 30 minutes talking about why he thought he might be beyond hope. After that we spent another 15 minutes talking smack to each other, belly laughing as we went. We both felt better.

I resisted the temptation to tease him and say yes as soon as he asked his opening question. I have literally known him all of his life - so I have plenty of evidence that he is a genuine sicko - in harmless ways that close friends tease each other about. I also know that he has had plenty of really hard things tossed his way, and some of them really derailed his life and living.

I could tell even before he asked the question that he was in a reflective state - maybe too reflective. His voice was deeper and slower than usual. He was questioning some deep things - about himself, about his past, but especially about his future. That last one was what I was most excited and encouraged by!

He is one year into a pretty significant life re-start. This is after years and years of a slow-burn death spiral - and I mean it. He almost died - and in his words - "from his own doing". But in the last year, he had been doing some major life renovation. It started with changing some of his habits - actually most of them. First he worked on physical habits that were affecting his health - that is why he almost died. After that he spent quite a bit of time working on his spiritual habits. And now, he is working on emotional habits. That is a great formula by the way - one I wrote about in my book *Emotalerting: The Art of Managing the Moment* (available on Amazon).

After he shared more thoughts on why he was thinking he was broken beyond repair, I immediately told him why I thought there was no way he was too broken to fix. It was really simple.

For one, he had a year of proof that he wasn't too far gone. He had successfully overcome many obstacles and bad habits and life choices. He had even restarted his career one week before this. And second, he was questioning whether he was too far gone or not. I assured him that if he was "too sick in the head to change" - his words again - then he wouldn't have called me and he wouldn't have been asking the questions he was asking.

I was pretty happy when we were done. I was honored that he called me - that he trusted me with his doubts, that he would let me life-coach him, and most of all that he was owning his brokenness and turning it into growth. And the biggest thing was he called me - he reached out!

Unfortunately, I don't think many men are reaching out to their male friends for help. Men aren't seeking help from anyone very often. They need help - we all do. Men have as many problems as the next person - male or female. Years of studies show over and over that men have just as many emotional struggles as women, but definitely seek help less often than women do.

And when they don't seek help, their doubts, questions and struggles spin around in their heads, and their hearts (because they have those too) like a blizzard until they think they are "too far gone to fix." And they let it go until the next blizzard churns up again. They never end up getting their doubts and issues resolved.

When having questions and issues like my friend, most men "act out". They work it out at the gym, or yell it out in an angry argument, or drink it out in a booze binge, or even sex it out with a meaningless sexual encounter. These only make it worse because now there are more unhealthy issues to deal with...except for going to the gym - that's almost always a good outlet - as long as you still do the real work of working out your other issues when you are done.

An alternative could be to reach out to a friend and ask if they have a minute to talk about something. Most friends will feel the honor of the weight of this ask and say yes. They may get nervous, thinking they won't know what to say. But a lot of the time, they will know what to say because they are your friend. If they don't, it is still ok, because when no one is listening to us, it is really nice to have someone who will - even if they don't have an answer.

This part of having gritty relationships with men is a bit difficult. We tend toward isolationism and we are Negative Neds - not Nellies since this is a man book. In my interaction with my friend, I practiced nine things that we all could practice to be better friends.

Listen first

In my garage I have a framed mission/vision/value statement. It came together for me 25 years ago on a personal spiritual retreat. It is a filter and a guide for my life. There are some great statements that I borrowed from people smarter than me. One of them is "People don't care how much you know until they know how much you care." I got it from my pastor in the 1990's. He got it from leadership guru John Maxwell. Apparently he got it from Theodore Roosevelt.[28] I don't know where he got it from - probably Jesus - but not directly since there was a bit of span of time between those two men.

All of us want to be heard more than we want to be preached to - especially by non-preachers we call friends. This holds even more credence when we come to appreciate the Negative Bias from above. In order to be better friends, we should have a hope for more of our friends. You are not endeavoring to be their counselor or psychiatrist, but friends always hope for better for their friends. But if we don't listen first, it is not likely that we will make any ground for them, or for our relationship with them.

Be Fully Present

Information consumes attention hence a wealth of information creates a poverty of attention.

- Herbert Simon - 1977 Nobel Prize Winner

Here's a quick experiment: If you are in a public place right now, take a look around you. Focus on people who are sitting together. How many of them are looking at their screens rather than looking at the people they are with? So who are they really with? Not each other.

Attention Impoverishment is a real thing these days. We are constantly enticed, bombarded and hijacked by information - a lot of it for the sake of entertaining us and making us feel good in the moment. I won't even get into the brain chemistry that activates while we are being informationally entertained…

---

[28] https://www.goodreads.com/quotes/34690-people-don-t-care-how-much-you-know-until-they-know

When we are having conversations with people, we need to remain present with people. We all know when someone is not really present with us - mostly because they are looking at their screen instead of us - how insulting is that anyway? The first practical tip to being fully present is - be fully present. Stay focused on your friend and not your screen - even if your screen is really small on your watch.

There are a couple of other things to remember so you can be fully present.

Listen Empathetically: Empathy means that we step into people's emotional realities instead of just observing them. This may sound anti-man - because it is concerned with emotions. But it is actually really masculine because empathy engages the thinking brain and the solving brain after it has engaged the emotional functions of the brain. Here is the quick and easy formula:[29]

- I understand what you are thinking - read people
- I understand what you are feeling - feel people
- I am concerned and think I can help - help people

It is really that simple. You can speak these statements out loud as you move through the conversation or you can play in the background.

3 elements of a good conversation:

- We give our full attention to each other.
    - We focus only on your friend.
    - We communicate nonverbally.

---

[29] Goleman, Daniel. Dan Goleman on Focus: The Secret to High Performance and Fulfillment. November 22, 2013. Intelligence Squared

- ▸ We lean slightly forward toward each other.
- ▸ We make eye contact.
- ▸ We track with each other by nodding our heads, saying "Ok" or "Oh" and making other audible sounds.
- We experience conversational synchrony.
  - There is a rhythm of connection in conversation - almost like a dance. People in a good conversation start to sync up. This is actually a brain activity called oscillation. It is where we mimic each other and simultaneously adapt to each other.
    - ▸ We nod at the same time.
    - ▸ We simultaneously finish a sentence together.
    - ▸ We laugh or cringe at the same time.
- We feel good.
  - When the conversation is over, even if it was hard, both people go away feeling good.
  - This also is a brain activity where the "feel-good" hormones of dopamine, serotonin, endorphins, and oxytocin are released. These hormones not only make you feel good, but they positively affect some of your organs and body tissues too.[30]

Ask questions more than you make statements

This is a logical follow-up to listening well. As you listen and hope for a better and different future for your friend, things will occur to you. Things you think they should try. People they should talk to. People they should stop listening to. Attitudes

---

[30] Watson, Stephanie. Feel-good hormones: How they affect your mind, mood and body. July 20, 2021. https://www.health.harvard.edu/mind-and-mood/feel-good-hormones-how-they-affect-your-mind-mood-and-body

they should adopt. Podcasts they should listen to. Books they should read. That is a whole lot of "shoulding" on them, so do it carefully and slowly. Don't rattle off that whole list at once.

Some of the secret sauce for meaningful conversations is imagining some cool and new stuff for them - things they probably want for themselves but are overshadowed by the clouds of Negativity Bias. Another one of my statements on my garage wall is that discovery is the greatest of empowerers. This means that telling people something has less power than people discovering things for themselves. So ask more questions. You may have things wrong anyway, so asking questions can clarify where they are and especially where they want to go. Then both of you make some good discoveries. Ask simple questions like:

- What about that is exciting?
- What about that frustrates you the most?
- Did that surprise you?

Even my ten-year old nephew knows the value of asking questions. A few months ago when we visited Idaho from our home in Arizona, he asked my wife "What is new in your life since last time you were here?" My wife was pleasantly surprised by the question and intrigued about how she might answer. She told him she had a new friend whom she was enjoying and getting close to. If a ten-year old can do it, you can too.

Foster a growth mindset for them

I would like to borrow a popular theory in entrepreneurial circles called "growth mindset versus fixed mindset".

Someone with a growth mindset views intelligence, abilities, and talents as learnable and capable of improvement through effort. On the other hand, someone with a fixed mindset views those same traits as inherently stable and unchangeable over time.[31]

This mindset differentiates success and failure simply by attitude and thoughts. Successful people consider the possibilities more than the predicaments they find themselves in. The opposite of this would be to shrink away from and submit to the unfortunate or even oppressive factors overshadowing them and their situations. Here are some aspects from each way of thinking, being and acting:

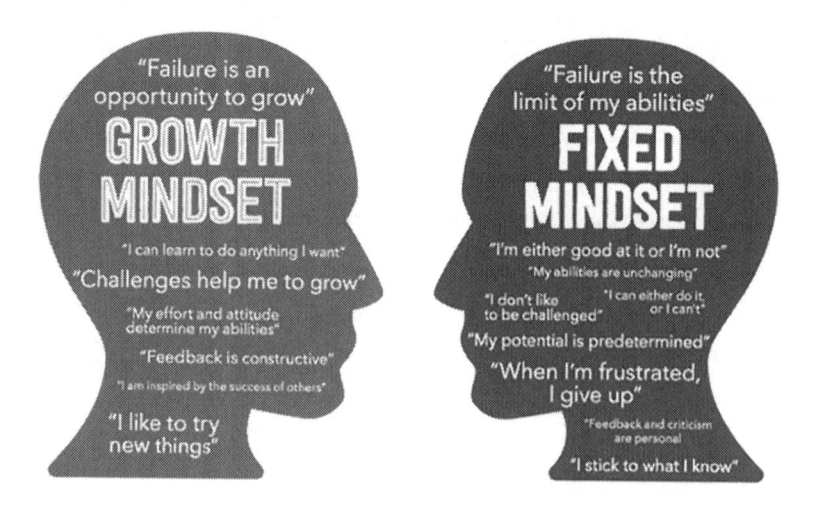

GROWTH MINDSET
"Failure is an opportunity to grow"
"I can learn to do anything I want"
"Challenges help me to grow"
"My effort and attitude determine my abilities"
"Feedback is constructive"
"I am inspired by the success of others"
"I like to try new things"

FIXED MINDSET
"Failure is the limit of my abilities"
"I'm either good at it or I'm not"
"My abilities are unchanging"
"I don't like to be challenged"
"I can either do it or I can't"
"My potential is predetermined"
"When I'm frustrated, I give up"
"Feedback and criticism are personal"
"I stick to what I know"

Source: https://www.its.vic.edu.au/blog-post/growth-mindset-vs-fixed-mindset-which-one-are-you/ March 3, 2023

Since we are predisposed to react negatively to regular parts of life and living because of the Negativity Bias, when we have meaningful conversations that change things for the positive, we have to remember where we are starting.

---

[31] Cote, Catherine. Growth mindset vs. fixed mindset: What's the Difference? https://online.hbs.edu/blog/post/growth-mindset-vs-fixed-mindset. March 10, 2022

This part of engaging meaningful conversation is something that runs in the background. This is more like a seasoning to the conversation - like salt and pepper. This isn't the first thing we talk about. We may never talk directly about it as a response to them as they download the particulars of their terrible day. How would you respond to your friend telling you that you need to develop a better mindset to offset your negative attitude when you just shared about your tyrant boss and heavy traffic?

Remember the Magic Ratio of 5:1

We have known this since the 1970's thanks to extensive research from a guy named Dr John Gottman. He coined the phrase "The Magic Ratio."[32] This concept got hijacked over time and was translated to five compliments for every one criticism. I have to admit that I have always struggled with this because it seemed too contrived - a little fake. I am a growth mindset person, so I am always looking at ways to help people move forward. So inserting compliments with a required quota while building a person up with growth challenges seemed like plactations turning into platitudes and it would interrupt the momentum of a meaningful conversation.

Imagine my relief when I discovered that Gottman didn't say to give five compliments for every one criticism. Gottman's study found that in conflict conversations successful couples had five seconds of time together in a positive (or neutral) emotional state for every one second in a negative emotional state.[33]

This is doable! And it is a great tool to help overcome, or at least neutralize the Negativity Bias. Remember, this chapter

---

[32] Kari Rusnak. Why the negative sticks and how to retain the positive instead. The Gottman Institute. The Magic Ratio: The Key to Relationship Satisfaction. https://www.gottman.com/blog/the-magic-ratio-the-key-to-relationship-satisfaction/
[33] Ibid

is not about how to create conflict conversations, but how to create impacting conversations that have the possibility of changing things. So the conflict is the human proclivity to be in a perpetual state of negativity to protect ourselves - aka The Negativity Bias. So if I have a 30 minute conversation with my friend, a total time of 6 minutes should be neutral or positive reinforcement - with a minute here and a minute there. I can do that. Pretty sure you can too!

Play Out the Worst-Case Scenario

We already know we have a strong disposition to think about and focus on the negative. So why not play it out? If the bad, hurtful, despicable and destructive thing we are imagining did happen, what would happen next?

- I will punch them in the face and kick them in the man-parts.
    - Cool. What happens after that?
- I will hurl demoralizing insults at them.
    - Good one. What do you think they will do in response?
- I will articulately tell them how wrong they are.
    - What do you think might happen next?
- They will see how much they hurt me.
    - Ok. What if they don't care?
- I will cut off all contact with them.
    - They sound like a sucky friend. That could be a reasonable solution moving forward. What things would that add or remove from your life?

Imagining a scenario that responds to the Negativity Bias will neutralize and maybe even disempower it because we thought out the worst-case scenario. This will engage the emotive parts of our brains. It gives them an environment to react that is safe but not real. It will then turn off and deactivate the parts of their brain that are alerted to the fight or flight mechanism in the interior brain. And then the cognitive, thinking parts of the brain will engage and rationally work through what happened and what to do next.

Imagine the Silver Lining

After imagining the worst-case scenario, a good next part of a meaningful conversation is to make some lemonade out of lemons. We've turned down or turned off the fight or flight parts of our brain and fired up the rational parts. We can empower this by practicing the Silver Lining Approach.

The principle that every bad situation produces something good or teaches some lesson. It is derived from the fact that clouds, even though dark, often have bright silver edges where the sun reflects.[34]

There's a spectrum to our thinking pattern, and every outcome you can think of lies on a range between two non-existent ideals: unrealistic pessimism - the worst-case scenario and unrealistic optimism - shangri la-land.

Unrealistic Pessimism	Realistic Pessimism	Realistic Optimism	Unrealistic Optimism[35]

A good goal is to get to somewhere in the middle with a healthy dose of realistic pessimism and realistic optimism, and it's best to have a healthy equilibrium of both.

---

[34] https://www.urbandictionary.com/define.php?term=Silver%20Lining. March 3, 2023
[35] Adriana Azor. Apr 11, 2020. How to Overcome Your Brain's Negativity Bias, https://medium.com/brainchronicles/how-to-overcome-your-brains-negativity-bias-a2acbc5352c9. Accessed March 2, 2023

Realistic pessimism dials down the Negativity Bias to actual reality. You can help them think through things like:

- Wondering what might be going on in other people's lives that are motivating them to do or say what they did or said to you.
- Remembering the changes in your industry or economy that are contributing to not getting a raise or, worse, getting laid off.

Realistic optimism promotes our beliefs in our capacity for growth by tapping into incredible potential. Realistic optimism helps us visualize what is possible (rather than impossible) to work hard towards making it a reality.

- What might be true, even a little bit, about what they just said or did to me?
- What's a little nugget of learning I can gain from what they said or did to me?
- I have learned a lot from this job. This could release better opportunities, including more life/work balance.

Scatter Simple Pleasures

Let's lighten it up a little. Having intentional conversation is, well, intentional. It involves paying attention to the current episode of your friend's life and doing something productive in it. This is active and it is work and sometimes it is intense. So where's the fun?

Insert the fun throughout the conversation. I tried to do that while I was writing this. It doesn't have to be hard. Actually, it is what we are good at as men - talking about light and shallow things like sports and weather. Crack little jokes. Make fun of yourself. Notice the song in the background and reminisce about what you were doing when that song came out. And then get back to the important and meaningful conversation.

This is conversational breathing. This is like taking a breath. Sometimes it is like catching your breath. Conversations need to be able to breathe. Conversations don't have to be a sprint or even a marathon. Sometimes you actually need to stop so you can take a bathroom break. All conversations have a life cycle. A beginning and an end and a middle. Allow for the ebbing and flowing of depth and shallowness. Neither should be the entirety of the conversation. Slow the pace for conversational breathing.

Landing the Conversation Plane

That brings us to the end of meaningful conversations. The most risky parts of a plane trip are the take off and the landing. Meaningful conversations are a lot like that. We've talked about the take off - seizing a moment to dive deeper into the life of your friend through a conversation.

So what about the end? You can ask a few easy questions (remember - ask more questions than you make statements):

- How are you doing right now? This is a better man-ask than "how are you feeling?"
- Where are you right now? This is kind of like a really quick recap or summary - not a regurgitating of the conversation.
- Where are we right now? This is a chance for you to make sure they won't suffer from "sharer's remorse". After you hear their answer, assure your friend that you are both

good. Let him know you respect him even more now that you know what he is going through. Thank him for being open and honest.
- What are a couple of take-aways you got from this conversation?

Then change the subject to something less intense - like sports or weather. Changing the subject will lessen the likelihood of them having "sharer's remorse because the last thing on their mind when they leave will be lighter and less intense or invasive.

BACK TO LAS VEGAS

This chapter started with me telling the story about my friend who texted me and asked me to call him. Let's call him Joe (a regular and average name even though I consider this friend way above average and splendidly irregular!). I told you about my response to his request and used it as a way to introduce the Negativity Bias that most humans live by and filter their conversations through. The Negativity Bias is a great thing to remember as we add value to our friendships, but hopefully you now realize that is only a starting point for meaningful conversations.

I want to circle back and tell you more about what Joe told me about - with his permission.

A long-time friend, let's call him Max, recently moved to the Phoenix area. The move was precipitated by a series of relationship losses. Max needed a fresh start. My friend, and one other friend, let's call him Ned, in Phoenix, are basically his last resort. They are mid-life three musketeers - the last three standing together as they struggle into mid-life together. Joe is pretty sure that Max doesn't have anyone else anymore and since Ned and Joe are in Phoenix, he moved there.

Joe and Ned have seen Max cycling down with a debilitating lifestyle and deteriorating relationships for a while. They have seen this first-hand since he relocated to Phoenix. Last week Joe and Ned decided that they could not sit idly by and watch Max keep disintegrating his life. So they showed up to his place unannounced. They sat down and engaged a meaningful conversation that called him and his destructive lifestyle out. Max listened. Max responded. He has a lot of work to do that he has only just begun.

Joe told me that at one point, Max shared that he was embarrassed that he was such a disappointment to them and that he didn't deserve their friendship. Joe only minimally acknowledged this self-deprecating gas-lighting and told him that he was stuck with them. He needed to make some changes and they were going to be there for the changes, through thick and thin. Knowing Joe, even if Max doesn't change, he will be there for him. He won't empower his bad decisions and lifestyle, but he will figure out what being there will look like - will live like. Max really is stuck with Joe and Ned.

These are the types of gritty relationships men should have. These are the types of relationships that are sorely and tragically missing today.

These are the types of conversations too many men are too afraid to have - so they retreat into the cowardly and shallow conversations where they only talk about sports and weather while they watch each other's lives circle the drain.

Stop being cowards. Engage gritty conversations!

DISCUSSION QUESTIONS

1. On a scale of 1 (low) to 10 (high), how influenced by the Negativity Bias are you? Have there been times when you were closer to 10? What circumstances tend to take you closer to a 1?
2. What are the strengths and weaknesses of the Negativity Bias?
3. How good are you at having meaningful conversations?
4. When have meaningful conversations jump-started you?
5. Are you more of a fixed mindsent or a growth mindset? What is the evidence?
6. What is keeping you from having more meaningful conversations?

5
Gritty Habits

Do you have any nasty little habits? I do - more than one. One of the worst for me is one that I don't ever remember not having. I don't know how I got it. I don't know where it came from. I don't know why it plagues me. Most people don't know about it because they don't see it. But I know some people know about it because they have noticed it. It is persistent. I have tried to break this habit over and over, but I always find myself slipping back into it. I don't really enjoy it even though a day doesn't go by that I don't slither up to the habit bar and order a regular, sometimes a double... It causes me physical pain sometimes - not a lot but a little - when I take it too far. It borders on self-hurting but not quite self-mutilation.

Have I built enough anticipation? I bite my fingernails! It's nasty. I hate that I do it. When I get my car washed, I am embarrassed because there are always fingernails on my car mat that they have to vacuum up. GROSS! When I talk to a person over coffee and point out something in a book or on a piece of paper, I cringe that they are seeing evidence of my bad habit. I could go on, but I think you get the point. I have a really bad habit.

We all have them. Some good - some bad. And we don't know why we have some of them or where they even came from. There are habits we don't have that we wish we did. Habits are a big part of our life and living - everyday. So much so that research suggests about 45% of our daily behavior is habitual.[36]

In this part of our journey toward being gritty friends, it's time to chat about habits and how we can help each other improve or remove activities of the body, mind, or spirit that hold us back or bring us down. One part of enjoying a deep, meaningful and gritty relationship is to help each other grow into some things we aspire to and grow past some things that are holding us back. Great friends help each other identify some habits to help us flourish while discarding ones that are neutral or diminishing.

WHAT IS A HABIT?

Here is a clinical definition:

> In clinical terms, habits are automatic. They are a bunch of repetitive responses learned by an organism for ease of living. When you face a similar situation repeatedly, your reaction to it becomes automatic. A habit is a settled tendency. Or you can even say it is an acquired mode of behavior, which either becomes partially or entirely reflexive. Habitual behaviors are usually unnoticed by those engaging in them.[37]

---

[36] Vanessa Gibbs | Jan 2 2023, https://www.blinkist.com/magazine/posts/break-bad-habits
[37] Habits I – Building Better Habits: Understand Habit Formation, and Take Control of Life, by Team DocVita | Nov 20, 2020. https://www.mayooshin.com/how-to-break-a-bad-habit

In less clinical terms, habits are all about ease and efficiency. Habits are shortcuts because they become automatic - so automatic that our brains do them for us without thinking. We just do them because they are providing something for us that can be done with little to no energy so our brain can focus on other more important things. "We want the brain to learn how to do those things without energy and effort," says Russell Poldrack, a professor of psychology at Stanford University.[38]

In addition to ease and efficiency, habits also have the value-added feature of bringing us pleasure and making us feel good - even about bad or unhealthy things. This pleasure sensation fires up in our brain and becomes physiological in that it creates a neurological pathway for chemicals or electrical impulses to travel down.

This is how it becomes automatic or habitual. Habits form without us trying to make them happen and most, if not all, habits make us happy - whether they are good and healthy habits or bad and unhealthy ones. Even bad habits make us feel good - at least in our brains and at least for a moment and maybe even for a few minutes. I cannot figure out why biting my fingernails makes me happy, or why other bad habits do too. But they do hijack what I consider sensible and healthy happiness with stupid and unhealthy, short-lived happiness that is quickly overtaken by remorse, irritation and determination to never do it again, until I am once again shaking my head in disbelief as my cuticle is bleeding from biting a fingernail on a finger that didn't have any fingernail to bite on - or whatever other bad habit I am indulging for momentary happiness.

---

[38] Shirtsleeve, Cassie. 5 Science-Approved Ways to Break a Bad Habit. TIME Online. August 28, 2018. https://time.com/5373528/break-bad-habit-science/

This epic struggle with bad habits is as epic as humans are. It is pervasive even in the Bible. I hit on it already in Chapter 2 in the story of Adam and Eve's first stumble into sin.

Another of my favorite portrayals of this is in Romans Chapter 7. I affectionately call it the "do-do" chapter. The Apostle Paul, a champion of Jesus and right-living (aka righteousness) tells us of his profound struggle with bad habits or sin.[39]

> [15] For I do not understand my own actions. For I do not do what I want, but I do the very thing I hate. [16] Now if I do what I do not want, I agree with the law, that it is good. [17] So now it is no longer I who do it, but sin that dwells within me. [18] For I know that nothing good dwells in me, that is, in my flesh. For I have the desire to do what is right, but not the ability to carry it out. [19] For I do not do the good I want, but the evil I do not want is what I keep on doing. [20] Now if I do what I do not want, it is no longer I who do it, but sin that dwells within me.[40]

Bear with me for a minute. I don't want to be sacrilegious, but what if I changed some words to bring it into the context of good and bad habits.

> For I do not understand my own actions. For I do not do what I want [good habits], but I do the very thing I hate [bad habits]. [16] Now if I do what I do not want [bad

---

[39] I am not saying all bad habits are sin. Many are. For instance, I don't think biting my fingernails is a sin. But it is gross, unhealthy, embarrassing and something I wish was not in my life. Whatever the Apostle Paul struggled with was more profound than biting his fingernails and he called it sin that killed parts of him. This is a good example of the power of a bad habit whether it is sin or not.

[40] Romans Chapter 7, Verses 15-20. English Standard Version.

habits], I agree with the law [God's law of righteousness or really good habits], that it is good [good habits]. [17] So now it is no longer I who do it, but sin [bad habits] that dwells within me. [18] For I know that nothing good [bad habits] dwells in me, that is, in my flesh [my body]. For I have the desire to do what is right [good habits], but not the ability to carry it out. [19] For I do not do the good [good habits] I want, but the evil [bad habits] I do not want is what I keep on doing. [20] Now if I do what I do not want [bad habits], it is no longer I who do it, but sin [bad habits] that dwells within me.

This is profound. This text is saying that sin or bad and unrighteous habits live in our bodies. And modern brain research has proven this to be true. Habits are a matter of ease, pleasure and physiology. They are also a matter of consciousness and virtues or at least they could be with some intentional practice at good habit-making.

So the struggle is real! The struggle with bad habits is profound and physiological and modifiable.

Many habits—including smoking or excess sugar consumption—involve the brain's dopamine (or reward) system. Dopamine is a "feel-good" chemical that transmits signals between neurons in the brain. The first time you engage in a new, "rewarding" behavior, you get a euphoric feeling from doing it as a result of a dopamine release, notes Russell Poldrack, a professor of psychology at Stanford University. This leads to changes in both the connections between neurons and the brain systems responsible for actions—and can largely account for why we start to form bad habits in the first place.[41]

---

[41] Shirtsleeve, Cassie. 5 Science-Approved Ways to Break a Bad Habit. TIME Online. August 28, 2018. https://time.com/5373528/break-bad-habit-science/

Once these brain-habits are made, they are hard to shake. But your brain is capable of forming billions of neural pathways that become habits. These pathways never disappear or even collide with each other. This will both blow your mind and make some new neural pathways. Humans have 100 billion neurons. Each one can connect to 250,000 other neurons. If you do the math, that is 25 quadrillion pathways. That is a lot of potential habits! That number is 25 with 375 zeros after it. Here is another way to think of how many connections your big brain can make:

> To give you an idea of how much that is, there are only about 250 billion stars in our milky way galaxy. So you have 1 million times as many potential neural pathways as the stars in our galaxy. Or, consider the Ara constellation, it's 24 quadrillion miles away (4000 light-years), and it would take us about 64 million years to fly that far with humanity's best current spaceship. And your brain has the potential for 25 quadrillion connections![42]

WE CAN CHANGE BAD HABITS

> *All bad habits start slowly and gradually and before you know you have the habit, the habit has you.*
>
> - Zig Ziglar - 20th Century writer, salesman and motivational speaker

---

[42] Neural Pathways: How Your Mind Stores the Info and Thoughts that Affect Your Behaviour. https://lifexchangesolutions.com/neural-pathways/.

The bad news about bad habits is that they require diligent work to be overcome by good habits. We create new neural pathways for good habits all the time. And once a new pathway is created, it remains. But so do the old habits.

It is like a hiking trail. When you come across a trail that is closed off for remediation/repair, in spite of the best efforts to conceal it, we can still see it because the pathway is still there. It is the same for habits. Since we can create so many of them, once they are created, they remain in the brain - once created, always created. We likely have heard the Alcoholics Anonymous mantra, "Once an alcoholic, always an alcoholic". There is truth to it. There is a propensity to return to old habits, be it alcoholism or finger-nail biting, because the pathway to the old habit exists - physiologically exists. It's actually a trail in your brain.

The good news for bad habits is that we are superheroes when it comes to the ability to make new habits. Even I could be a former fingernail biter instead of once a nail-biter, always a nail-biter. We have a unique advantage over any other created being. In everyone's neural system there are tons of spindle cells. Those are the cells from where new neural pathways are created. And like I said, we have tons of them. And they stick with us well into old age. In fact, we have way more spindle cells than any other creature. We really can teach an old dog new tricks!

In my first book about emotional intelligence[43], I spend a lot of time on this neural stuff because it fascinates me and answers a lot of questions of why we do some of the things we do that we don't like about ourselves. While I was doing research for the book, I simultaneously did some of my own research. I did a year-long study on 100 subjects to see if emotional intelligence

---

[43] Emotalerting: The Art of Managing the Moment. Available on Amazon.

correlated with spiritual formation. There were lots of things that were interesting and surprising. One of the biggest discoveries from my test subjects was how emotions, and the reasons we have them, can be divided into three categories. Emotions are a response to one of three unmet needs:

- Physiological - We need things. These needs are our basic and instinctual needs for food, shelter, relationships, and actualization/that we matter. We expect people to at least acknowledge our needs for these things. If people block our way to them, we get emotional.
- Intellectual - We need to know things. We learn things that are more than instinctual. As we learn them, we value them and incorporate aspects of them into our living. If people disrespect what we have come to know, we get emotional.
- Spiritual - We need to believe things - especially good things that are bigger and more important than us. These are things like religion or politics - the things we are not supposed to talk about because we can lose our composure when they are doubted or questioned. If people discount what we have come to believe, we get emotional.

I'd like to apply this to our habits and even call them "habit-ats" - where our habits are at - where they live. Let me ask some questions about your habit-ats:

- Which of the three do most of your daily habits revolve around?
    - Meeting physical needs
    - Meeting intellectual needs
    - Meeting spiritual needs

What percentage of your daily habits are in each one?

I think most people have a breakdown close to 60/30/10. 60% Physiological; 30% Intellectual;10% Spiritual or somewhere close to that. You certainly don't have to agree with me on the percentage, but I really do think this is the breakdown. This is not scientific. I have done no research to support it. I just base it off 30 years of life coaching and pastoring. I really do think this is the order. Most of our habits support physiological lives. After that, our habits support our intellectual lives. And finally after that, our habits support our spiritual lives.

This order is interesting and maybe even a bit odd since if we get challenged on any of these, the opposite happens with our emotions. We get way more offended when people oppose our religious convictions or political ideations than we do if they take the last brownie at the gathering of friends where religion or politics happens to enter into a discussion.

This is what I am saying.

Most of our habits focus on physiological habits that we have mostly dialed in. We are getting the biggest percentage of those needs met with not a lot of effort because we have the habits to support them.

As a distant second, when it comes to intellect, how many habits do you have to expand your knowledge base and stimulate your brain? How many books have you read this year? Book reading is on the decline and is lower now than it has been since the 1990's.[44] Instead of books, we rely on the internet for quick answers which may or may not be correct. We rely on podcasts that may or may not be more than personal opinion seasoned with passionate rhetoric inspired by personal hurt or

---

[44] https://news.gallup.com/poll/388541/americans-reading-fewer-books-past.aspx. Downloaded March 6. 2023.

pain. I love to learn through podcasts.[45] I love being able to do responsible research for this book with the internet. But I have certainly had to set up some systems in my life to have a steady input of education into my busy and comfortable life.

Then, a distant third are the habits that bolster our spiritual lives. When it comes to beliefs, how many beliefs do you have where your beliefs are challenged with action and not just internal, visceral passion. How often do you put something at stake for your spiritual beliefs? If you really believe them, shouldn't you have to live them out and not just keep them on the inside? How have you lived out your beliefs respectfully but sacrificially in a culture that cancels out those who live with convictions that are different from theirs? And are any of these actually habits, or are they something you check off a few times a year? If we really believe something, they find their way into the way we live and we will have habits to support it.

The bottom line is this: Most of our habits perpetuate our needs. Less of our habits increase our learning. Even less of our habits are convictional enough to enlarge the world around us.

What about your bad habits? What percentage of your bad habits feed those same three categories I presented earlier? For me, I think the same formula and percentage breakdown applies. Most of my bad habits center around basic physiological needs. For instance, every single morning, I begin my day with coffee, meditation and stretching in my jacuzzi on my back porch. This is a good habit. A not so good habit is how often I indulge my love for sweets. I eat way too many carbs and I have a gut to prove it. I am going to share a way I am working on my habits this year, inspired by a meaningful conversation with a friend (Chapter 4!). Unfortunately, none of these goals/habits I am

---

[45] I do listen to podcasts everyday, but I am careful to know why I listen to them - to strengthen my views, values,and beliefs - even if they are not aligned with the podcaster.

working on this year addressed my sugar habit. I may need to revisit my goals for this year.

As I move out of considering my physiological habits and move to intellectual ones, there are less bad habits centered around my learning. I have some good ones regarding reading books and listening to podcasts. I have a lot of bad learning habits centered around random scrolling on my phone. I gain a lot of education about things I really don't need to know or that are negative and feed dark sides of me that shouldn't be fed.

When it comes to beliefs, I have a lot of habits for that. I am a pastor so I get paid to learn and apply spiritual things. I am pretty lucky (or blessed as I like to say) on that front. But I don't think the average person spends enough time investing in their spiritual life so it can be lived out in their community. I have to be careful there too. I can read about leadership and theology all day long, but if I am not applying it for the benefit of my relationships and my community, it is only for self-edification.

AN EXAMPLE OF HABIT-AT GOALS

Late last year, I was having an unplanned conversation with one of my staff members. He is a pretty goal-oriented man. He retold me about a conversation he had with one of his friends about goals for the next year. They heard of an easy system that came up with a few major and measurable goals for the year that could be reported on a wall calendar with a check mark. When the day's goals were met, a check mark would be made on a calendar. I loved the idea and modified it to reflect some daily habits I wanted to focus on that would further my goals for the coming year. I color-coded each habit/ and made a check mark for each color when I practice/complete each habit. Here they are:

- I am loved by God. I will watch for his love today. Did I pray with focus for 15 minutes today? (B)
- I am a follower of Jesus. Did I watch for ways to follow Him today? Did I do a devotional or Bible study for at least 15 minutes today.(B)
- I am a pastor. Did I watch for ways to shepherd people today. Did I pour into someone today? (B)
- I am a teacher. I will watch for ways to teach today. Did I research or teach today? (I)
- I am a learner. I will watch for learning opportunities today. Did I read a book or listen to podcasts for 20 minutes today? (I)
- I am a writer. Did I write for at least 2 hours this week? (I & B)
- I am an artist. I will watch for and create art today. Did I play the piano for 30 minutes this week? (P,I & B)
- I am a triathlete. Did I complete my prescribed training regimen today? (P)

Before I did this, I knew I wanted to have a more specific plan for some things but had not taken the time to formalize them into a plan that created or tapped into habits I either had or wanted to have in my life.

I don't know if you noticed how many of these had to do with the last two habit-ats of intellect and belief? How many of them had to do with the first one of physiology? That is what the letter at the end of each one means. Here is my breakdown:

- Physiological goals/habits 25%
- Intellectual goals/habits 50%
- Belief goals/habits 63%

Before you question my mathematical abilities, which are the lowest of all my intellectual abilities, the number is greater than 100% because some habit-ats have more than one designation. So cool your math-jets!

So you can see that I am heavy on the Intellect and Belief habit-ats. I have less stated goals/habits associated with physiology. That is likely because those habits are pretty deeply ingrained in my daily routines and these habits and goals were areas I wanted to up the ante on this year. Although, I do think I am going to amend my goals as I approach the second quarter of the year in a few weeks and add something about my bad habit of excessive sugar/carb consumption. Maybe I should also add something about finger-nail biting...

I offer this as an example of how to set and evaluate habits in your habit-ats. Let's move to how friends can help friends with good and gritty habits. Here are five things to consider so you can develop and maintain good habits for yourself and for your friends.

Don't be afraid to judge, just don't be judgemental

There is a basic difference between being judgemental and judging. Judgementalism is about demeanor and attitude. Judging is about facts and observable behavior. Gritty friends have a responsibility to comment on the observed behavior of their gritty friends. Although, the methodology is important. If you are mightier (I would never do that) and holier (how could you do that) than thou, your friend is a lot less likely to listen to anything from you. A real fact is that too many men are walking around with no one helping them make good choices and good habits that strengthen them, their families, their careers and everything else that they actually have control and influence over, if only in their response.

When you broach the subject of a bad habit, say something like, "I may be off, but I've noticed [behavior, attitude, etc]. Is that something you want in your life?" Or if they have mentioned to you that they want to work on something, you can say, "I remember that you mentioned you wanted to do better at [behavior, attitude, etc]. The other day I noticed...." And don't forget to give them kudos when you see them keeping the reins tight on a bad habit that is changing into a good one!

Habits have a life cycle

All habits are activated and lived out in the same way: Cue, Routine, Reward.

- Habits start with a cue or a trigger that the brain recognizes. This recognition takes place in the interior part of the brain and happens automatically in response to the environment. Example: I am stressed from a hard day.
- Routine is how the habit is acted out in your current situation/reality. You respond in the same way with very little variation to the same or similar cue - that is why it is called a habit. Example: When I am stressed, I like sugary treats.
- Reward is the positive outcome of the habit and becomes the intrinsic reason for the formation of the habit. Example: Sugary treats make me feel good for a few minutes and interrupt my stress.

When it comes to altering/improvising good habits or overruling bad habits, the order is reversed. When you are talking with your friends about your or their habit that may require a change or be deleted altogether, take a look at what the reward may be. What is that habit providing for your friend and is the reward a healthy habit? If the reward is not or less than healthy, then a change of routine has to change in order to change the brain response. You have to create a new neural pathway and lay down some pavement by repeating the new routine. This does take some time and it will probably be longer than three weeks like I was always told.[46] On the average it is more like 9 weeks at the low end and 36 weeks at the high end.[47] So be patient and be persistent.

Let Old Habits Die

There is a saying I learned early in church work: dismount dead horses and give a funeral if needed. This means that when a ministry has served its purpose, acknowledge its contributions, but if it isn't serving people's needs or maturing them in their faith, don't do it anymore.

Brain research shows how ingrained habits are in our physiology and even in our psychology. But studies also show that there is a part of our brains that are devoted to overruling old habits that don't have use anymore and making that determination happens moment-by-moment.

A study at the Massachusetts Institute of Technology[48] used rats and chocolate milk - who knew rats liked chocolate milk so much. In essence the findings of the study suggest that the infralimbic cortex [part of the thinking center of the brain

---

[46] This became popularized in the 1970's and can be traced back to Dr. Maxwell Maltz, a cosmetic surgeon and author of "Psycho-Cybernetics" (Prentice-Hall, 1960). In his book Maltz reported that his patients needed a minimum of 21 days to change the mental image of how they looked.
[47] Lally, Phillips et.al. How are habits formed: Modeling habit formation in the real world. 16 July 2009. https://onlinelibrary.wiley.com/doi/abs/10.1002/ejsp.674
[48] Trafton, Anne. How the brain controls our habits: MIT neuroscientists identify a brain region that can switch between new and old habits. October 29, 2012 https://news.mit.edu/2012/understanding-how-brains-control-our-habits-1029

- rather than the center parts of the brain where habits are activated] is responsible for determining, moment-by-moment, which habitual behaviors will be expressed.

This means that we can decide in our thinking brain, not our reacting brain, that an old habit is old and not useful. And when we see a friend falling back into an old, ineffective habit, even in the moment, we can remind each other that a certain habit's use has had its day but it is no longer a part of how to live healthily.

REPLACE OLD HABITS WITH NEW ONES

A really good way to replace a habit is to replace a bad habit with a good one. The human brain is really receptive to this.

Instead of trying to stop doing something—"It's hard to stop a behavior," says Berkman—start doing something else.

"We are action-oriented creatures," says Berkman. Some studies have shown that the more you suppress your thoughts, the more likely you are to think about that thought or even revert back to that bad habit. A 2008 study in Appetite, found that those who suppressed their thoughts about eating chocolate exhibited a behavioral rebound effect, where they consumed significantly more chocolate than those who didn't. Similarly, a 2010 study published in Psychological Science found that smokers who tried to restrain their thoughts about smoking wound up thinking about it even more.

If you're a smoker and you tell yourself not to smoke, your brain still hears "smoke," Berkman says. Conversely, if you tell yourself to chew gum every time you want a cigarette, your brain has a more positive, concrete action to do, he notes. Similarly, if 5 p.m. has been linked with a glass of wine for years, use it as a time to, instead, double down on hydration and make sure the fridge is stocked with seltzers, cold water and lemon, Berkman says.[49]

What we focus on becomes what we habituate towards. This is true even in how we talk to ourselves and each other.

Speak About Who You Want To Be

"A powerful agent is the right word. Whenever we come upon one of those intensely right words...the resulting effect is physical as well as spiritual, and electrically prompt."

- Mark Twain (quoted by William Dean Howell in "My Mark Twain")

Self-talk can be really important and impactful when you are trying to replace a bad habit with a good one.

In order to replace a bad habit with a better one, use the words "I don't" instead of "I can't." Instead of saying things like, I can't eat sugary treats, use decisive, victory language like "I don't eat sugary snacks. Or I eat sugary snacks on Friday night and it's Thursday night. Or for my plaguing habit, "I used to bite my fingernails, but I don't anymore."

This is a little more than positive self talk. It is backed up by studies. In a research study published in the Journal of Consumer Research, 120 students were first split into two different groups

---

[49] Shirtsleeve, Cassie. 5 Science-Approved Ways to Break a Bad Habit. TIME Online. August 28, 2018. https://time.com/5373528/break-bad-habit-science/

to study how they withstood temptation.[50] Here is a summary of what they discovered:

- To test the students' ability to resist a chosen temptation, one group was told to repeat the phrases "I can't", and the other to use the word "I don't."
  - For example, if presented with chocolate, one group would say "I can't eat chocolate," while the other group would say "I don't eat chocolate."
- Each group was then asked some quick questions unrelated to the study. But, when they walked out of the room, they were presented with two complimentary treats—a chocolate candy bar and a healthy granola bar.
  - Surprisingly, the researchers found that the students who used the phrases "I can't" chose to eat the chocolate candy bar 61% of the time.
  - Conversely, the students who used the word "I don't" only chose to eat this 36% of the time.
- Another similar study was also conducted on a different group of 30 participants split into three groups. This time the same experiment would test the impact on the phrases on their health goals.
- After 10 days of research, they found that only 1 out of 10 in the "I can't" group were able to stick to their goals.
- In contrast, 8 out of 10 in the "I don't" group were successful in meeting their goals.

---

[50] Patrick, Vanessa M. and Henrik Hagtvedt (2012), "I Don't" versus "I Can't": When Empowered Refusal Motivates Goal-Directed Behavior," Journal of Consumer Research, 39 (2), 371-812].

WORDS ARE IMPORTANT

Words do more than say things. They change things. Gritty friends help their friends grow and change. This includes carefully and compassionately challenging their habits that are undermining productive, growth-oriented and healthy living. Let's help each other dismount the dead horses we are trying to ride around. In that spirit, I leave this chapter with a story dedicated to forging new habits with new horses.

A cowboy's horse died on his way to town. As he was walking down the dusty trail, he happened across a ranch. With a renewed sense of hope, he asked the stable keeper if he had any horses for sale.

"Sorry, I've fallen on hard times myself. I had to sell all of my horses!"

The cowboy noticed a rather strange-looking steed standing right in the stable behind the keeper, a horse with matted, mangy fur, a deranged, glazed-over look in his eye and a stiff, motionless stance that would have made him look more like taxidermy than a living animal if it hadn't been for the occasional twitch.

"How much for that one?" the cowboy asked.

The stable keeper shook his head. "Trust me. You do NOT want that horse. I got him from a real shady-lookin' preacher one day. I don't know what that man did to him, but all's I know is that the horse ain't right. Never has been."

The cowboy had his doubts, but he was desperate, and insisted on buying the horse despite the stable keeper's warnings. The keeper let him have the horse for free, as he couldn't bring himself to charge money for such a defective creature in good conscience. Before sending him on his way, the keeper gave the cowboy some instructions:

"As I said, this horse ain't right. He's completely unresponsive to everything except for two specific sentences. To make him go, you have to say 'Thank you Jesus!' To make him stop, you say 'Hallelujah!' In all honesty I can only hope the Lord is riding with 'ya tonight, 'cause otherwise... Well... Just be careful, okay?"

The cowboy excitedly hopped on his new horse, ready to ride off into town. Remembering what the old stable keeper told him, he shouted "Thank you, Jesus!" and instantly the horse went from standing to top speed in a second, nearly giving the cowboy whiplash!

Onward the horse galloped, smashing into fences and bushes that didn't slow it down for a second, dashing in a straight line even after missing its first turn a long time ago. It almost seemed a miracle that there were no trees directly in the way, because the horse would have surely run into one.

The cowboy instantly regretted his decision, and in his panic he'd forgotten which phrase made the horse stop. Then, to his horror, he realized that the horse was heading full-speed off the edge of an incredibly steep cliff. The cowboy began frantically pulling on the reins, screaming all the religious phrases he could think of to try and halt the beast, but to no avail. Suddenly, when all hope seemed lost, he remembered at the last minute:

"HALLELUJAH!!!"

And instantly the horse froze, a single inch away from the edge of the cliff.

The cowboy was trembling and drenched in sweat. He had never been so close to certain doom. With a sigh of relief, he wiped his brow, looked up to the heavens and said:

"Thank you, Jesus!"[51]

---

[51] A cowboys horse died on his way to town. https://www.reddit.com/r/Jokes/comments/9wws85/a_cowboys_horse_died_on_his_way_to_town/. Downloaded March 7, 2023.

For the record, after writing this chapter, I have not bitten my fingernails. A lifelong habit overcome by a new habit - of not biting my fingernails.

Here's to learning new habits well, and quickly!

DISCUSSION QUESTIONS

1. What bad habits do you have? What makes them bad? How did you acquire them?
2. Are your most irritating bad habits more slowly connected to meeting physical needs, intellectual needs or spiritual needs? How hard is this to determine? Why?
3. What are some intentional habits you would like to create? Why?
4. Do you speak to yourself more about who you aren't or who you would like to be?
5. Who are some friends you could ask to help you with your new habits?
6. What friends can you offer to help with their habits?

6
Gritty Accountability

A body of men holding themselves accountable to nobody ought not to be trusted by anybody.
— Thomas Paine - American Revolutionary Activist

I sabotage myself for fear of what my bigness could do.
— Alanis Morissette - Singer, Songwriter, Actress

...I do not understand my own actions. For I do not do what I want, but I do the very thing I hate...I do not do the good I want, but the evil I do not want is what I keep on doing.
— The Apostle Paul - Romans 7:15 & 19

THE ART OF SELF-SABOTAGE

I was watching a spy action series the other day. One of the villains said something that really got my attention. "Humans have the uncanny ability to sabotage things that are really in their own best interest." The villains used this really common human tendency to zero in on their victims. I think, too often, we are the villains zeroing in on ourselves.

Last week, I enjoyed having coffee with a friend, Chuck, (made up name) whom I hadn't seen in a few years. We used to meet every week for years - challenging each other to be better men - to become gritty men. Then a few things shifted in our relationship. I moved out of the area which made it hard to meet regularly. He also needed some specific help for an area in his life where he was self-sabotaging. For him this self-sabotage was directly related to something he didn't want to do. He didn't want others to do it either. He started a not-for-profit organization to help others stop acting out self-sabotaging addictions. Yet he himself was secretly flirting with the same self-sabotaging activity he was helping others not to engage in. It ended up causing him to shut down his not-for-profit. Confusing, Right?!?

As we caught up on less invasive things like marriage, jobs, and hobbies, I jumped into the deep end. I directly asked him how he was doing with "the thing" that had been keeping him from being the man he wanted to be - the man God wanted him to be. He said he had been "clean" for over three years. He found specific help to get to the core of his self-sabotage. For him it was shame. His discoveries took some time and were complicated, but basically, he was raised in such a shame-based environment, that he had a hard time not living in an environment where he would not have shame. So he created opportunities to potentially feel shame.

Isn't that something? I told him it was insidious. It was sneaky and damaging and prevented him from being the man he wanted to be, the man he felt called to be. But he was no longer a self-sabotager. It was really good to see him and to see him self-actualizing instead of self-sabotaging. He was definitely more gritty!

WHY DO WE SELF-SABOTAGE

The reasons we self-sabotage are usually complicated and often-times trauma-based, so it is not easy to get a succinct answer to why we do it. But I came across a really good and simple one: We self-sabotage because we have learned that it works really well.[52]

This means that self-sabotage has given us something that provides a solution to something that makes us challenged or uncomfortable. Or the pain of self-sabotage is less than the risk of pain we are already experiencing. Self-sabotage provides a solution for discomfort - even if it is only in the short term, and even if it is unhealthy and destructive in the long-term. Self-sabotage helps us cope with our present realities.

To counter it, we have to realize what self-sabotage provides and then counter it with better alternatives. Here are some examples:[53]

- If you want to stop abusing alcohol, you need to compassionately understand that alcohol "works" to alleviate your stress after work.
- If you want to stop stress eating, you need to compassionately see how stress eating "works" to make you feel less lonely in your unhappy marriage.
- If you want to stop procrastinating, you need to compassionately understand that procrastinating helps you avoid fear of failure or fear of success.

---

[52] Wignall, Nick. Self-Sabotage: Why You Do It and How to Stop for Good. June 7, 2020. https://nickwignall.com/self-sabotage/
[53] Ibid

In each of those scenarios, the solution is self-actuality rather than self-sabotage. Imagine a different means for the same solution.

- How can I relieve work stress in a healthy, productive way - like going to the gym or taking a brisk walk with my dogs who need exercise as much as I do.
- How can I remedy loneliness in my marriage - like having dinner together and talking about each other's day or about what you're each learning about yourselves.
- How can I counter procrastination by admitting my fear but then taking a step toward my goal anyway.

HOW DO YOU SELF-SABOTAGE?

Here is a list of common reasons for self-sabotaging from Forbes Online.[54] Which one is your sabotage-de jour?

- **Procrastination:** Putting something off and making excuses, is a common self-sabotaging behavior. Excuses are made to attempt to justify an unnecessary delay that prevents you from reaching a goal. For example, you might put off studying for a test because you fear failing, or you might tell yourself you don't have time to meet with a nutritionist, so you can't work on eating more healthy this month.
- **Courting Temptation:** You can self-sabotage by putting yourself in a situation that tempts you away from meeting your intended goal. For example, an individual who

---

[54] What Is Self-Sabotaging, And Am I Doing It? Silva, Lauren. October 7, 2022. https://www.forbes.com/health/mind/what-is-self-sabotage/

struggles with substance misuse and who is in recovery chooses to go to bars to hang out with friends, even though they could spend time elsewhere.
- **Reprioritization:** Some individuals may replace an intended activity or goal with another obligation. An example of this might look like someone saying, "I was not able to go to class this semester because I had to take care of my sick neighbor."
- **Self-Medication:** Some self-saboteurs may unconsciously turn to overusing drugs or alcohol as a way to avoid working through difficult emotions or thinking about past trauma.
- **Perfectionism:** High standards are one thing, but perfectionism can lead to self-sabotage if you end up setting standards for yourself that are impossible to reach.
- **Defensiveness:** Self-saboteurs may hide emotional weakness under a strong and/or happy mask. These people may get defensive when others try to get close to them. Defensive self-saboteurs may have difficulty living in the present moment and end up pushing people away to avoid getting hurt emotionally.

STOP SELF-SABOTAGING

If you want to stop self-sabotaging, use the words I started with: Humans have the uncanny ability to sabotage things that are really in their own best interest. Ask yourself: Is this activity serving or undermining my best self-determined or God-determined interests? If it doesn't advance one or both, then stop doing it, unless you want to keep self-sabotaging.

One of the best antidotes to self-sabotage, as well as laziness, temptation, arrogance and a slew of other things that keep us back from our best future is to be accountable. Here is an assessment I adapted from a celebrity/corporate America Life Coach and relationship expert named Patrick Wanis[55]. Take a few minutes and answer these 14 questions on a scale from 1 - never, 2 - rarely, 3 - sometimes, 4 - usually, and 5 - always. Don't be over-analytical.

1. Do you frequently say "I know"?
   - Never, rarely, sometimes, usually or always?
2. How often do you lean on the wisdom of others and not just on yourself?
   - Never, rarely, sometimes, usually or always?
3. How often do you admit, "I don't know"?
   - Never, rarely, sometimes, usually or always?
4. Do you easily admit when you make a mistake or are wrong, or do you easily become defensive or deny you were mistaken?
   - Never, rarely, sometimes, usually or always?
5. Rather than seeking to blame others, how often do you own your own actions or outcomes?
   - Never, rarely, sometimes, usually or always?
6. When faced with feedback or criticism, do you welcome it and consider it for improvement, rather than making excuses and becoming defensive, offensive, or belligerent?
   - Never, rarely, sometimes, usually or always?
7. Are you reliable and dependable?
   - Never, rarely, sometimes, usually or always?

---

[55] Wanis, Patrick. https://www.patrickwanis.com/14-traits-of-immature-men-who-run-from-responsibility-and-accountability/

8. Do you keep your word?
   - Never, rarely, sometimes, usually or always?
9. Do you understand your roles and responsibilities?
   - Never, rarely, sometimes, usually or always?
10. Do you embrace the reality and ramifications of your situation even if it's bad and you mostly caused it?
    - Never, rarely, sometimes, usually or always?
11. Do you have a growth mindset more than you have a fixed mindset? (A fixed mindset avoids challenges, reacts harshly to mistakes; a growth mindset embraces challenges, learns from mistakes, and focuses on growing and developing skills and intelligence.)
    - Never, rarely, sometimes, usually or always?
12. When faced with a problem, do you focus on the solution, rather than focusing on finding the culprit and then complaining and blaming?
    - Never, rarely, sometimes, usually or always?
13. Do you openly learn from errors and mistakes, while imagining a new way to do things and adjust behaviors?
    - Never, rarely, sometimes, usually or always?
14. Do you believe you are accountable to anyone? -Never, rarely, sometimes, usually or always?

The lower your score, the more you could benefit from an accountable relationship with a friend. The higher your score, the more responsive you would be to an accountable relationship.

Now, to get the most out of this chapter, give these same questions to one or two of your closest friends - your spouse or girlfriend can be one of them. Ask them to evaluate you. Tell them to be honest and assure them there won't be any negative repercussions from their answers. Hopefully there will be positive ones because it is likely you can learn a thing or two from their evaluations.

And as you get through this chapter, hopefully you will be hankering to invite a friend into an accountable relationship and you can begin with these questions.

WHAT IS ACCOUNTABILITY

I have noticed lately that there has been an increased cry (more like a roar) for accountability. From what seems like a lot of chaos in our world, many of us are looking for the reasons for the chaos. And when the reasons don't change anything, people look for "accountability".

But is that really what people are crying out for? Are they looking for responsibility or accountability? There is a difference between being held responsible and being held accountable. Responsibility has more to do with an action that was taken by an individual or a group/organization. Accountability has more to do with the outcome of the action. Responsibility can be delegated and assigned. Accountability cannot. The one who took the action is the one who took the action. The only part of responsibility included in accountability is that the person who took action is responsible for the outcome and any effects it has - positive or negative.

Is accountability destructive or constructive, or both?

In the Old Testament of the Bible there is a really good verse about the mutual reciprocity of accountability. Here is the verse: *As iron sharpens iron, so one person sharpens another*. One way to view this nugget of wisdom is to understand that in order for iron to sharpen iron, one has to be harder than the other - or the two metals would chip away randomly at each other without purpose or fashion. In order for iron to sharpen iron, one has to be heated to pliability while the other stays colder and harder. The one that is heated is sharpened by the other. When it comes to accountability, it is the same. One is heated up - with life and its difficulties or bad choices and their ramifications. The other comes alongside and chips away at the heated iron to make it even sharper - rather than duller. In gritty relationships, sometimes one friend is the hot, pliable, and shaped iron while the other is the cold, strong, shaping metal. Good friends know when they are the shaped and when they are the shaper. But both become sharper in the process! Good accountability is both destructive and constructive.

Accountability for a lot of people only means punishment, retribution or penalty. In our culture of chaos, when people say they want people held accountable, most of the time they really mean they want the one who had responsibilities for the planned action to pay a price for the outcome - usually at a sacrifice.

Accountability can also be positive. If accountability is about outcomes, then when an outcome is positive, we like to see who produced it. We also know that a lot of people clamor for credit for good outcomes, even if they had no real responsibility or contributed to any outcome.

Good accountability is proactive. It is constructive. It is preemptive. There are aspects of accountability that can be retributive, but the goal of the retribution is to move a person to a better future through accountability.

Another problem about accountability is that most people aren't really very accountable - in the areas of life that matter. They matter because of how they connect to community and not just the individual. The areas of life that matter include the interior areas of a person that end up getting addressed somewhere and somehow in community. What we seek out will leak out - always. The things done in secret will always connect to communities and relationships. You cannot convince me otherwise.

Whether or not you agree with me about that, the world around us has plenty of evidence about the effects of anonymous, non-accountability. Unfortunately, even in churches, there are many indicators of the destructiveness of non-accountable men and women and how those shallow, non accountable relationships lead to detrimental consequences that always affect community through marriage, children, neighborhoods, churches, companies, etc.

Howard Hendricks, a pastor, theologian, and seminary professor, studied 237 instances of Christian men (mostly Christian leaders) who experienced moral failure. There was one common factor: not one of the 237 had accountability relationships with other men.[56] It validates one of my life mantras in my Life Mission that I have hanging in my man-cave: Personal isolation leads to personal desolation.

Accountability for men and women is not the same. For women, accountability is really different. They seldom call it accountability. The reasons are interesting:

> There's an invisible natural law in the female "culture" that helps to shape how women interact with other women at work and in their personal lives. It's called the "power dead-even rule," a term coined by Pat Heim

---

[56] WorldWide Family, Inc. https://www.northwestu.edu/assets/documents/watchmen/Oct2012-wgmf-accountability.pdf. 2011.

and colleagues in Hardball for Women: Winning at the Game of Business.[57]

This is how the "power dead-even rule" works for women:

- Rules govern relationships, power and self-esteem (not just for women)
- The "power dead-even rule" means that in order to have a healthy relationship, the self-esteem and power of one woman must be, in the eyes of each woman, similar in weight to the self-esteem and power of the other. In other words, these key elements must be kept "dead-even."
- When the power balance gets disrupted (such as a woman rising in status above other women), women may talk behind her back, ostracize her from the group or belittle her.
- These behaviors help to preserve the dead-even power relationship that women have grown up with their entire lives.
- Of course, this is a subconscious process. Most women are not aware of this invisible rule and what drives their behavior, but it is a big reason why women sometimes do not support other women.

There are other rules for women and many of them are reasons closely attached to women in the work-force rather than women in friendships.

---

[57] Andrews, Dr Shane; Why Women Don't Always Support Other Women https://www.forbes.com/sites/forbescoachescouncil/2020/01/21/why-women-dont-always-support-other-women/?sh=39eb346f3b05

I did my own informal study by calling some women in my church and asking them why they don't have "accountability" relationships. By and large, they simply have relationships where accountability flows from as a byproduct of the relationships. But they seldom, if ever, call it accountability. They call it a relationship.

Men tend to have accountable relationships that are formed specifically for accountability and relationship follows. The order is reversed. Or men have relationships that are activity-based (hunting, mountain biking) and information-based (news, sports, hobbies).

In summary,

> "female friendships tend to be more dependent on face-to-face contact, are more emotional, include the sharing of thoughts and feelings, and include more support. Friendships between males tend to be more side-to-side rather than face-to-face. Males tend to value relationships that include shared activities, are less intimate, and transactional."[58]

For men, what does accountability look like? For men, as I said, it is usually activity or interest-based. It can move to accountability when men begin to enjoy each other's company not just because of the activity. They become interested in each other's lives and well-being. They start to care about each other's internal and external lives. Once this starts to happen, accountability is a logical relationship next-step.

---

[58] Bates-Duford, Tara. Ph.D. January 26, 2018 https://psychcentral.com/blog/relationship-corner/
2018/01/female-vs-male-friendships-10-key-differences#1

No Regrets Ministries, a Christian-based leadership training/equipping organization has a good definition of accountability: "Giving others the freedom to help you order your private and public lives."[59] This is a really good definition whether you are a person of faith or not. I'd like to take a look at the components in Sonderman's definition.

- **Give -** Permission for good and effective accountability has to be granted. For accountability to be the most effective, it can't be forced. This means it can't only be church recommended for morality purposes, government sanctioned for penalty and rehab purposes, or wife mandated for "or else we're getting a divorce" purposes. Notice I said "only". It could start that way, but if it stays that way, it won't last long.

Accountability "opens the door for men to be pressured, cornered, and coerced into admitting what they really don't want to admit."[60] If you want to help your friend with accountability, you have to offer it, not demand it. Accountability for men can never be forced or taken if it's going to be internalized, impacting and meaningful. It has to be a little kinder and gentler than that. It has to be offered more than it is demanded. It has to be given, like a gift being offered, and so it can then be received by the recipient's choice and free will.

- **Others -** If we were our own best accountability partners, we would not have to be held accountable! The reason we

---

[59] Giles, Kirk. What is Accountability and How Do We Develop This Relationship?. July 6, 2021 https://www.impactus.org/articles/mens-ministry-what-is-accountability-and-how-do-we-develop-this-relationship/

[60] Men: Seek Transparency Rather than Accountability. September 18, 2021 by: Ray Ortlund. https://www.crossway.org/articles/men-seek-transparency-rather-than-accountability/

need accountability is that there is something blocking our best practices, preferences and dreams in the first place. Therefore, any effective accountability is given to us by others. When we enlist the help of others we are giving them a couple of important permissions:

- License to Observe - Since accountability springs from relationship, chances are you will have some sort of relationship that gives your accountability partner an opportunity to observe you in a variety of settings; formal and informal, planned and spontaneous; when you are at your best or at your worst.
- Somebody's Watching Me - I am an 80's teen! I really love 80's music - everyone should! There was a one-hit wonder by artist Rockwell in 1984 - a collaboration with Michael Jackson. Here are some of the opening words:

    I'm just an average man with an average life
    I work from nine to five, hey, hell, I pay the price
    All I want is to be left alone in my average home
    But why do I always feel like I'm in the Twilight Zone[61]

    I would say the reason the man in the song is paranoid and living in the twilight zone is because he is isolated and content with only an average life (tongue duly inserted into cheek). After all, personal isolation leads to personal desolation!

- **Freedom to Help** - Today's "you do you" culture is pervasive.[62] I happen to think it is very destructive to both individuals and to community. In this live and let live mantra is a hyper sensitivity to observation and

---

61 Source: LyricFind; Songwriters: Kennedy Gordy; Somebody's Watching Me lyrics © Sony/ATV Music Publishing LLC
62 This was written in the early 2020's.

evaluation. Offering help is viewed as judging and is vehemently condemned. Last time I checked, that would be a decidedly contradictory, judgmental posture. Accountability has to have some flow and freedom. Keeping some of these ground rules in mind will help:

- **Judging and judgmentalism are two different things.** Judging is evaluating observable behavior. We judge our surroundings virtually every waking second - usually for safety or pleasure. Judgmentalism is all about delivery. Judgmentalism is usually abrasive, condescending, retaliatory and destructive.
- **Accountability is an offering, not a demand.** When we observe behavior or attitudes that may undermine our friend's dream and goals, we offer the observation and maybe a recommendation. We cannot demand that they accept either the observation or the recommendation. We cannot make our friends do a single thing. We can appeal to their own desires and dreams. Posture it as a thing on the palm of your hands that you extend to them. They can take it or leave it. You're just offering it. Once you retract your palms, it either falls to the ground or they take it into their own hands. You simply offer it - they receive it or dismiss it.
- **Accountability is a receiving posture.** My mother used to nag me about standing up straight - I had bad posture. Accountability partners are not your mother, but they may tiptoe up to the "nagging" line, and sometimes even step over it. The receivers must remember that they want help from someone who sees some actions or attitudes that could be getting in the way of their hopes and dreams - they

see us slouching in some way. A defensive posture is contrary to accountability.

- **No Gossips Allowed.** Trust is elemental to accountability. There are no gossips allowed in accountable relationships. Borrowing the Las Vegas tourism motto from 2003 is appropriate here: "What happens in Vegas, stays in Vegas." This was used for permissive partying without accountability - which is the opposite of what we are talking about here. But the privacy part of it does apply. Confidentiality is a sacred ingredient for accountability to work. So is authenticity and honesty. The only time confidentiality should be broken is if your accountability partner is threatening harm to himself or others - and even then you have to tell him that you are taking it to the next level to get them help so they don't hurt themselves or others.
- **No Drama Kings Allowed.** Many times in accountable relationships, when we share we are just venting - letting off the steam of emotion. Be happy that you or your friend are expressing some emotions - the thing we get accused of not doing as much as we should. We may say things we don't mean with some potency fueled by the emotion of the moment. Don't escalate the situation by adding fuel to a flaming emotional fire. Remember that you carry a squirt gun of gas and a squirt gun of water. If you squirt gas on an emotional fire, the fire gets bigger and hotter. Squirt a little water on it. This usually happens simply by listening. Don't throw a bucket of water on it - that could kill the moment and any future sharing that is deep and meaningful. But also, don't

minimize emotions while your friend is expressing or experiencing them. You can squirt a little water by asking a 1-10 question. I do this all the time. On a scale of 1 (low) to 10 (high), how upset are you, or how important is this to you in the big scheme of things. After a few hours, or the next day, check in on that number again.

- **Accountability is Action-Oriented.** Accountability has to be more than astute observations and well-meaning recommendations. It has to include action steps. Think of it as a punch in the shoulder (confronting) and a pat on the back (encouraging) at the same time. Accountability partners don't just punch or pat - they do both. If it is an actionable step, it is observable and measurable. That means you can verify whether or not you did it. And those steps should be small steps, not large ones. Change is sustainable and long-standing when it is made in small increments.[63]
- **Accountability is experienced through reciprocating relationships.** One of the best parts of accountability relationships is that they are two-way improvement projects. As you come alongside your friend, they are simultaneously coming alongside you too. You are holding each other accountable at the same time. You both get challenged. You both get scrutinized. You both get encouraged. You both get stronger. If accountable relationships are only one way - where one person is always the advisor, those are mentor relationships. Mentor relationships have

---

[63] Read Atomic Habits by James Clear for an excellent presentation of how to change, make and keep good habits.

a place in our lives, but the dynamics and purpose are different from those of accountability relationships.
- **Order -** Do you ever have deep ponderings with inanimate objects without brains? There is one inanimate mindless thing that gives me fits on a regular basis. It's my backyard hose. How does it get so tangled and knotted? There was this one time when I was watering some parched yard plants in my backyard, and I couldn't quite reach the intended target. I pulled and the hose would not give even an inch more. I got frustrated and started to lose my mind and pulled really hard. You know when you lose your mind, you have extra special Neanderthal strength? That happened. What I didn't know is that the hose was not knotted. I was pulling the hose from the spigot. My Neanderthal strength got the best of me so much that I bent the pipe at the spigot where it was attached to my house. I couldn't believe it. I tried to bend it back and ended up breaking the pipe at the new Neanderthal-created, metal crease. I had to turn the water off for the entire house and call one of my friends to come and fix my Carlyle-created disordered drama.

Do things like that ever happen to you - not with hoses, but with your life and living? It could be because of frustration or lack of power and control, but whatever its source is it leaves you subjected to disorder when you want order.

One of the aspects of accountability that we all have to remember is that accountability is a response to chaos. Accountability strives to bring order to disorder. Your life is filled with order - we strive for it and get Neanderthal when disorder rears its ugly head - no matter what it looks like - hoses or people or insecurities or [insert your triggers here].

In churches, we used to set up tables for groups that help with specific problems (i.e. divorce, abuse, substance abuse). No one would stop by these tables because stopping by was a public admission of having a problem - unless people "were asking for a friend". Accountability is a little like stopping at one of those tables. You have to be willing to:

- Admit that your life has disorder - regardless of its source
- Admit that you could use some help reordering it
- Subject yourself to reordering and let a trusted friend come alongside you.
- **Private life -** This is a really big elephant in the living room of accountability - you're only as accountable as you want to be. There are things in your private life that really shouldn't be totally private. If you have secrets in your life, then the reasons are almost always bad. If there are things you are keeping to yourself, ask the question why that is. Secrets usually kill parts of us - both on the inside or the outside. Secrets kill little bits of you on the inside and they kill little bits of people you care about on the outside, like your spouse, your family and kids, your friends.

    Ask yourself: "Am I keeping secrets? Why am I keeping them a secret?"

    Ask your friends: "Are you keeping secrets? Why are you keeping them a secret?
- **Public Life -** All the world's a stage, and all the men and women merely players.[64] This is really true. Granted,

---

[64] Shakespeare, William. As You Like it, Spoken by Jacques.

maybe you aren't acting all the time, but people are watching all the time. People see your life. People see how you act, what you say, what you don't say. What are people seeing when they see you?

How do you react to your wife, your kids, your boss and your traffic? How do you behave when your way gets blocked? Are you a pompous butt or a passive manipulator? How do you talk with your unaccountable friends when they share crude jokes or put downs at the expense of people who aren't in the room and can't defend themselves? Is it easier to let the less noble parts of yourself rule the moment than the more noble parts of you? When you talk to your wife or kids, do you build them up or tear them down?

An accountable friend notices these things. And they do more than notice, they bring them up. They challenge a friend to add these things to their list of accountable personal improvement goals.

THE SHORTEST ACCOUNTABILITY MEETING EVER

Do you remember my friend Chuck I introduced you to in the beginning of this chapter? I want to tell you more of our story. Chuck and I first met at a coffee shop. We were both pastors, and for pastors, time in coffee shops is listed on our job descriptions as office time. We didn't know we were both pastors at first. We just kept seeing each other reading thick books and doing mindful work on our computers - we knew it was mindful work because our brows were furrowed most of the time - another part of the job description for pastors. I am pretty sure he initiated the first conversation. Our undercover pastor moments were over. We started talking regularly. Then we started meeting regularly. Then we started hanging out once in a while outside of the coffee shop. Our wives even met each other. We had become friends.

Soon enough we turned our regular meetings into accountability meetings. We used an acronym that spelled SOAP.

This, by the way, is an easy formula for you to follow in your accountability meet-ups. This can be your easy check off list - your agenda. Make some small talk and about 5-10 minutes into it shift to this list!

S was sacred - We would talk about things we held as sacred - non-negotiables in our life and things we knew we had to keep making better. Sacred to us meant Godly, biblical, and non compartmentalized - everything was open for questions and discussion - even (especially) the things we were struggling with - whether that was God, church, our wives, or ourselves. Each week we would check in with each other about the sacred thing we were wrestling with the most.

O was Observable - We would throw out observable actions or behaviors we were committing ourselves to for the following week so our sacred things would indeed be sacred and would also be better.

A was accountable - We held each other to the standard or goal we had set for ourselves the last week. Did we do what we said we would do? Sometimes we would even have some penalties we would exact on each other - ones we had agreed upon when we presented our "O". I remember one of mine was that I could not go mountain biking the next time I had time to go.

P was personalization. For us, that would usually be praying together right then and there. But it was also how we would be committed to remembering what we were working on that week and we would check in with each other, not just at our face-to-face meeting.

We met every week pretty much without fail. It was pretty rich, challenging and impacting.

One week, Chuck met me in the parking lot of our lunch place. We didn't even make it into the restaurant. He told me he couldn't meet because he had an appointment he had to make because he "was in trouble."

And he was. To make a long, sordid and disturbing story short, he sent a lurid picture of himself to a lady who ended up being a minor. He really was in trouble - with really serious ramifications.

We kept meeting each week. We just had a whole lot more to talk about - not just how he plummeted so deep into lust and pornography that he was having online sexual relationships. We also had to talk about why this had not been a part of the deep, rich, honest accountability I thought we were having. I learned that a person is only as accountable as they are willing to be.

The day finally came when the investigations ceased and he got arrested. He didn't know exactly when it would happen, but he knew it was going to happen soon. I'll never forget that day. Even as I write about it I start to tear up. Seeing his mug-shot on the local Phoenix area prime-time news was shocking and heart-wrenching. It was dramatized, but it was also true. He had done a really bad thing that he was now being held accountable for - being held accountable with a penalty of jail-time, not missing a mountain bike ride.

He was released on bail, but was confined to his home which was enforced by an ankle bracelet. We kept meeting each week. His trial came. I testified on his behalf speaking about his remorse, his repentance and his character that he was determined to refine and restore.

He went to jail. I visited him there too. He got out of jail. We kept meeting. He successfully worked on his state-mandated rehabilitation. We kept meeting. He successfully requested to be removed from lifetime probation. We kept meeting. He started a not-for-profit organization to help men with sexual dysfunction and pornography addiction. My wife and I served on his board. We kept meeting. He stumbled, not illegally, but morally. He regathered his footing. We kept meeting so he could regather his moral footing, but we did close up the not-for-profit. Eventually I moved out of the area. It was only then that we stopped meeting. By then he had formed some deep and meaningful relationships with men he could be accountable to.

It was a deep and meaningful relationship that changed us both. It was relationally rich and expensive at the same time. It took a lot out of us and put a lot into us. It was awkward and comfortable. It was fun and it was sad. It was disappointing and full of hope. We got to be there for each other. I am so glad we got to travel with each other through some tough stuff. Accountability changes people. Accountability reforms and transforms people. Accountability is worth it. Too many men make bad decisions and form bad habits because they are not accountable. Too many men can't get help when what they've done gets exposed. And instead of working through it toward healing and restoration, they retreat even deeper into solitary dysfunction, unhealth, and darkness.

Be a better friend. Be gritty together. Add lasting value to your male friendships. Reach out to a friend today. He is probably isolated and unaccountable and carrying around the burden of loneliness while he keeps treading the water of mediocrity in his life while the current of moral, social, and relational morbidity is sucking him into the deep.

Personal isolation leads to personal desolation!

DISCUSSION QUESTIONS

1. Have you ever had a friend pay a high penalty for keeping secrets?
2. Are secrets killing parts of you, parts of your marriage, parts of your parenting, or parts of your heart? What would it be like to have life in those places again?
3. What scares you the most about being accountable to someone? What scares you the most about NOT being accountable to someone?
4. Who comes to mind when you think of having an accountability partner? Why not give them a call and invite them to coffee and talk about this chapter with them?

7
Gritty Emotional Intelligence

I am supposed to be somewhat of a relationship expert. The bane of my relational existence is my relationship with a member of my nuclear family. I haven't been in fellowship with this person for nineteen years. This brings me a little bit of grief and a whole lot more relief. The relationship was always codependent and toxic. I think of this person often. I pray for her when I think of her. I wish no ill-will toward her. We may be related through genetics but there is no fellowship - no getting together for coffee or for any family gatherings, for a meeting of the minds or the hearts. That part of my family has no family gatherings anyway, so I don't even have to avoid or decline any gatherings.

The last time I was with this person was for one of my birthdays. As was the norm, our dinner conversation quickly turned toward her, her world and my contributions to it. It really was a conversation about my non-contributions to her world - all of the ways I had let her down, disappointed her and did her wrong. I didn't recall any of the instances the same way she did. It was long, wrong, irrational, confusing and damaging. Towards the end, when it was time to drive me back to where I left my car, she suddenly flipped a switch (which was the usual formula for our conversations) and said, "Oh, you didn't get to open your birthday card with your gift in it. Why don't you open it now." She was driving, so I could have safely opened it in front of her. I calmly replied, "The conversation we just had for two hours was really negative and I am not in a good space. I don't want to open it right now because it will taint the intent of the gift." To that she replied, "You are such a woman...". I explained to her I wasn't a woman, that I was a man, and a pretty masculine one at that, and that this was the last time she was going to be able to talk to me that way. And it was.[65]

Culture widely regards the expression of emotions as a feminine trait more than a masculine one. The fact is that men experience emotion as much as women.

Now scientists have just revealed another area where we get emotion completely wrong. Despite centuries of stereotypes, a new study finds that men are just as emotional as women. Men have the same ups and downs, highs and lows as women do.[66]

Men may experience emotion as much as women, but they don't express it in the same way. Men experience emotions internally with physiological responses like increased blood pressure and cortisol responses. Women have internal responses too, like increased depression and anxiety. Women are more likely than men to express their emotion in language and relationship rather than anger and aggression which are men's usual outlets.[67]

---

[65] I did offer to pay for therapy with a therapist of her choice so we could work through our issues. She declined. We have not had any conversations since.
[66] Escalante, Allison. Men Are Just As Emotional As Women, Study Suggest. November 12, 2021. https://www.forbes.com/sites/alisonescalante/2021/11/12/men-are-just-as-emotional-as-women-says-new-research/?sh=6ec0eb6f2e96
[67] Chaplin, Tara M. Gender and Emotion Expression: A Developmental Contextual Perspective. June 16, 2015. https://www.ncbi.nlm.nih.gov/pmc/articles/PMC4469291/

I recently experienced a pretty similar stereotypical reaction to masculine emotion in a conflict a trusted friend and colleague and I were having with another man. The disagreement culminated in a face-to-face conversation. As the conversation began, the guy who was disagreeing with us began to communicate articulately as his lips quivered. Through the course of the conversation we weren't making much progress until, at the end of the conversation, he shared some of his emotional triggers that shed a lot of light on why we were disagreeing. My friend and I were able to more clearly understand the background noise/context that was fueling the disagreement. Before the sit down, my friend and I commented that his points of contention seemed really emotional and not very factual and seemed less than masculine. Looking back, with the end of the conversation as context, we understood why his lips were quivering.

There were two parts of the conversation I left dissatisfied with - besides that the best we could do was agree to disagree.

- Why didn't he share the emotional part of his story that was fueling the disagreement sooner?
- Why did my friend and I so quickly discount his reactions to us as feminine - even before we had the face to face?

There is one answer to both questions.

MEN DON'T LIKE TO BE IDENTIFIED AS EMOTIONAL

Men are as emotional as their counterpart females are. But they express it differently. Emotion is a lot like a leaky pipe - eventually the water comes out somewhere and there is usually damage left behind, and the damage is unsightly until it is repaired.

Men are also identity seekers. Identity is defining and important to both genders, but a little more so for men. Men see identity as a measure of worth and value. Right or wrong, strength is a high determiner of worth and identity for most men. And right or wrong, emotion is too widely seen as the opposite of strength. An emotional man is seen as a weak man. And no man wants to be identified as weak.

About the same time as I was having the disagreement I described a few paragraphs ago, I was having another disagreement with a good friend and fellow leader. (I know - it sounds like I am hard to get along with - but really I am a leader, life coach, and pastor - leading people where they aren't likely to go on their own or they wouldn't be talking to me - so conflict is part of that formula). I was talking over the issues of the disagreement with my accountability partner (remember the last chapter?!). He pointed out that the other person needed to remember that he was dealing with a person that has trauma triggers. He was referring to me!

I actually didn't appreciate it at first. It was a label, and while it could help my friend that I was disagreeing with, I didn't want it to be my identifier. The issues of disagreement from my end were real and not informed by trauma. In my masculine world, being a triggered-trauma-guy was a weak identifier, not a strong one a leader should have. I decided that, when given the chance to work through the disagreement with my friend, I would leave that part out. I would not be vulnerable to my good friend (who I feared was about to become a less-good friend) about the triggered trauma responses I was having as a part of our disagreement. When I did get to hash out the disparity in our relationship, I came clean and shared that some of our disagreement was fueled by some trauma triggers.

I have always been an oxymoronic anomaly: athletic and artistic; relational and strategic; emotional and pragmatic; extroverted and introverted. All of those conflicting worlds have seemed to meet comfortably in the middle somewhere. But that being said, I did not want to be categorized as a person with trauma triggers. I didn't want that as a part of my identity and I didn't want the disagreement to be boiled down to me and my trauma triggers. I could see my headstone - my birthdate and death date and my epitaph that read "a trauma-triggered man, husband and pastor".

I was doing the same thing as my friend and I were doing with the man we categorized as "not masculine." I was doing it to myself. I was avoiding attaching something emotional to me or my identity or my worth.

MEN ARE EMOTIONALLY IGNORANT

Ignorance is remedial; stupidity is not...

I have seen this a million times: When you ask men and women, but especially men, to use feeling words, most of the time they start using other words - fact words instead of feeling words. When I ask people to use feeling words instead of fact words, that usually throws them for a loop - especially men. They have a hard time coming up with feeling words like frustration, rage, disappointment, defensiveness, outrage, disgust, fear, joy, happiness, hope, delight, etc. Anger is the go-to emotion for men. And anger usually gets emotionally expressed as an outlet for another emotion that preceded it - one of those on the list I just shared.

Most men know when they are feeling angry because anger is one of the categories of feelings they have been given language for. It came from people around them — mothers, fathers, teachers, coaches, peers, etc.

Imploring men to "express their feelings" without assuring that they have the tools to do so becomes more of a bullying type of put-down rather than a helpful request.

The problem for men, however, is not toxic masculinity, but rather incompetent or incomplete masculinity. Older men have failed younger men by not teaching them how to express themselves. Older men have failed to provide a language for younger men that will open their experience.[68]

Men can learn to be emotional and masculine at the same time!

SOMETHING IS AT STAKE

More than a decade ago, I formed a mentor relationship with a friend of a friend. Actually, it was a friend of my boss at the time. Even more actually, this man was an elder in the church where I was employed as a pastor. So indirectly he was on the team that was the boss of my boss. I was the protege. He was the mentor. The nature of our relationship was spiritual and theological. We would read deep and important books and discuss them while we ate lunch together - every two weeks. It was a sweet season of learning and growing and applying deeper truths to my life and my life's work - the church.

Oftentimes we would discuss more than the books we were reading together. At that time, I was a competitive endurance mountain biker - competing in local Phoenix

---

[68] Signorelli, Anthony. Hold Men Accountable: Move Beyond "Toxic Masculinity. SEP 13, 2021. https://medium.com/change-becomes-you/hold-men-accountable-move-beyond-toxic-masculinity-ba587c6ba0fc

races. I loved training for them and I loved competing in them. That year I was doing pretty well individually in a local race series. I was in first place in my age group! During the course of conversation, I admitted to him that before each race, I would always end up puking. He kept asking questions. He was good at that - right before he would make a poignant statement with another poignant and invasive question. I told him I puked because I would get really nervous before a race. It was really that simple. It wasn't that big of a deal - maybe a little embarrassing - but I usually went off somewhere where no one could hear or see me. I'd puke, recompose myself and then race. Then he dropped THE question:

"I wonder what is at stake for you?"

"What? I just get a little nervous."

"A little nervous, "he answered. "You are having a physiological response to a mountain bike race. It sounds to me like something is at stake."

And so a mini-quest began - to find out what was at stake for me when I ventured out onto the trails to compete with other men doing the same. To make a long story short, I came to realize that, due to some mommy issues (aren't they all due to some mommy issues...?), what was at stake was my masculinity. We talked more about that over some more lunches - and I got cured! I quit puking before races. And even now, before triathlons, I don't puke. I cough a little, but it stops way short before the dreaded puking.

For most men (and women) most of the time in relationships, there are things at stake.[69] Some are more obvious than others. And when something is at stake, emotions get involved - always. It is a physiological fact. We are constantly, even when we are asleep, evaluating our surroundings for comfort and for threats. Outside data comes to us from a multitude of sources and our sophisticated physiological systems evaluate them all - especially the threats. In the initial stages of this evaluation process, this outside data is evaluated in the internal, center part of our brains. The amygdala and hippocampus are the main processors of this data. The amygdala reacts first. Its response is very reflexive. It triggers the fight or flight or freeze response. (Usually it's one of the first two). After the initial evaluation, the hippocampus, which has base memory recall, scrutinizes the threats as real or ancillary and escalates or deescalates the reaction. For instance, wherever you are right now, if a door slammed, you would evaluate whether or not to duck under the table in nanoseconds. Your brain recognizes the sound of a door slamming and knows that it is usually not life-threatening, and keeps you doing whatever you were doing when you heard the door slam. You take a quick look to confirm that it's benign and keep doing what you're doing.

These series of responses are cool and really masculine! But what most people don't realize, especially men, is that the emotional life lives in this system. Your emotions react in the very same way - with all the memories too! This means that when something happens around you, you have emotional responses too - to pretty much everything that is happening around you. And it happens in nanoseconds - your emotions get

---

[69] This remaining portion of this chapter is summarized from a two-year research study I completed for my doctoral dissertation in 2013 and my subsequent #1 best selling book I published in 2015.

triggered in nanoseconds! That is the essence of triggers and of trauma. They are in your brain. And your sophisticated response system filters emotional threats as much as slamming-door threats. And when something reeks of an emotional threat, you trigger with emotions as much as you trigger with your body. Unfortunately for the man, the go-to response is anger.

Anger appeals to men because they can be angry and still remain well-defended and not vulnerable. Being angry not only helps many men to feel more in control of their own emotional experience but also use anger in an attempt to control their partner's expression of feeling as well.[70]

Learning how to be emotional may seem like a foreign language to most men, but it can be boiled down to learning what is at stake and quickly processing the perceived or real threat and triggering or deescalating it.

FIGURING OUT WHAT IS AT STAKE

When people start to "feel" emotional, it is usually because of a perceived threat - something may be at stake. Keep in mind that a perceived threat could be real or imagined, but definitely felt. Feelings are a part of the base-brain activity, not immediately overseen by the cognitive thinking center of the brain that could tame the emotional response with some rational thinking processes. There is an easy way to move from the irrational emotional realm to the rational thinking realm.[71]

---

[70] Weiss, Avrum, Ph.D. Men and Anger: You are angry, but you might also be scared. November 3, 2019. https://www.psychologytoday.com/us/blog/fear-intimacy/201911/men-and-anger

[71] This is the author's proprietary prescription for emotional stability and is informed by his own research and is discussed more thoroughly in his first book - Emotalerting: The Art of Managing the Moment and his doctoral dissertation on Emotional Intelligence and Spiritual Formation.

There are three basic components of healthy human existence that we seek and once sought, that we protect. They are satisfied in order and protected, which means one can only happen if the preceding one is satisfied. And all three have emotions that are independent and interdependent - feeding off each other and getting stronger at the same time.

- **What you need:** Basic human needs like food, shelter, safety, rest, acceptance and attachment.
- **What you know:** After basic human needs are met, humans seek out knowledge to keep the system that keeps their needs intact and sustainable.
- **What you believe:** After we come to know things, we develop values, beliefs and convictions that sustain the first two. The systems of this last one are things like lifestyle, religion, and politics.

The first component is the most important and is protected most vigilantly. The second one is pursued after the first and is protected accordingly. Finally, the third one is pursued and protected after the second one but not at the expense of the first one. Although when all three are present, there is a simultaneous homeostasis and interdependence. They all dance together at the same time. At that point, all three are protected. Any one of them could encounter a perceived threat and emotional reactions are likely to ensue as a reflex. The first one is more about survival, and is a function of surviving. The second is more about achieving a state of thriving. The third one is about sustainability - especially in the long-haul - handing off to others or offering a legacy so our existence matters in the long-haul of humanity.

As a person progresses through these they become more entwined and sophisticated and the responses are more emotional. This is why people have a hard time talking about religion and politics which is level three. We become more passionate about religion and politics when we have come to know more about both and after we know where our next meal will come from, where we will eat it and where we will lay our head down for sleep that night and not be lonely tomorrow when we wake up. This is also why, as we age, we get less tolerant of perceived threats to all three, because we want to protect our legacy since we sense our time is coming to a close.

So the first step to understanding and stabilizing our emotion is to identify which of the three components of mental processing is being threatened.

Ask yourself these questions:

1. Am I feeling threatened about some basic human needs like attachment, acceptance, or even food or shelter (if you perceive your job/livelihood or reputation as being threatened)?
2. Am I feeling threatened intellectually? Is someone questioning what I have invested time and energy to become knowledgeable about or become an expert about?
3. Are my values, beliefs or convictions being challenged, questioned or attacked?

At this stage, you sense that your emotion has become activated. It might be a rise in blood pressure or an increasing sense of irritation or frustration. It may or may not be elevated enough to cause you to be overtly emotional or angry.

It is not likely that you are being attacked by an evil person or that you are in the middle of some sort of an invasion by a control-freak. It is way more likely that these are more of an infringement. They will only become an attack or invasion if you keep letting yourself elevate emotionally - and you'll be the one on the attack.

- If you are experiencing a "needs' infringement, it will likely have to do with something physiological or psychological. It will be a perceived threat toward your basic human needs for safety and security. Safety and security needs are more physiological in nature and could be an infringement of your comfort or preferences - even for food or environment. Security needs could also be more psychological in nature and could be an infringement of attachment/isolation or acceptance/rejection by a friend or social circle.
- If you are experiencing an intellectual infringement, it will likely have to do with something you have come to know as true. It could be some knowledge newly acquired through experience or education, or it could be knowledge you acquired years before that is integrated into your lifestyle - including healthy and unhealthy emotional or physical habits. Intellectual infringement could come from something as simple as a question for data's sake that we perceive as a questioning for validity's sake.
- If you are experiencing a values, beliefs, or convictions infringement, it will likely have to do with something you have decided to believe or value. This is subjective, not objective. Is it subjective to you because you have decided to believe it (or not believe it) or you have

decided to live it out as a value and to have convictions about it? This is an ideal, culture, or worldview that you have integrated into your living. It may or may not be a mainstream view and is open to individual adoption. When people talk about politics or religion, this is a common area of this type of infringement. People easily become emotional if their values, beliefs or convictions are disrespected or condescended.

Now that your emotion has been activated, you get to manage it or it will manage you. You can quickly try to determine if you are feeling threatened/infringed on in your needs, your intellect or your beliefs, values or convictions by asking these three questions:

1. Am I sick, tired, hungry, lonely, isolated or otherwise physically or relationally compromised?
2. Am I highly engaged in a project, highly involved in decision-making or being highly intellectually stimulated?
3. Are my values/beliefs/convictions being threatened or ethically challenged?

In this phase you internally question your own emotions. You are attempting to determine if there are other underlying factors to why your emotions may be rising. This does not release the culpability or responsibility of the person pushing your buttons, but it can lessen the offense. After all, your buttons are your buttons - even if they pushed them. People seldom come at us with the intent of making us emotionally incontinent so we have a negative interaction and harm each other. Most emotional elicitations are unintended and unstrategic and are almost always just an attempt at self-comfort or self-adulation for the offender. Their part is their part, but you can only affect change in your part of what is going on. Your response-ability is your responsibility.

- *Needs Infringement:* If you are experiencing a needs infringement, you may simply be physically compromised. You may need a snack or a nap or both. You may be uncomfortable in your setting. You may be intimidated by the person or the subject. You may still be mad at your spouse for saying something or not doing something you expected them to do earlier in the day.
- *Intellectual Infringement:* If you are experiencing an intellectual infringement, you may be in the middle of a highly engaging process that has stimulated the cognitive parts of your brain. You may have learned something, researched something, solved something, or become informed by something that allowed you to make a decision or take some action. And you are in the decision-making or problem-solving mode because you have already subdued and overtaken barriers and blockers. You are in slay-mode. It would be like riding a really good wave on a surfboard. You're actually already surfing and the people around you are only paddling out. It is difficult to get off of the board while surfing to allow others to catch the same waves we are already riding to shore.
- *Beliefs/ Values/Conviction Infringement:* If you are experiencing a values/beliefs/convictions infringement, you could become emotional by a simple statement about something you have developed a belief about. To you, it is more than an opinion. You believe it and value it and have convictions about it. Someone you are talking to says something that conflicts with your predetermined

set of beliefs, values, or convictions. They may even want to debate about it, and for you there is nothing to debate because you have already decided. Maybe they just want to express their own beliefs/values/convictions to you or those around you. We are all entitled to do so. But sometimes we can hold our beliefs/values/convictions so tightly that even a question or random statement can be perceived as a questioning or a dismissal when it really was just a question or a statement.

After you have realized you are getting emotional and are now wondering what may be contributing to it, you can start to manage your response from a more even-keeled perspective. This is like an interception or an interruption of unbridled emotion that can damage the interaction or the relationship. Here are three more questions to ask:

1. Is this need logical or feasible in the moment? Is this person the appropriate person to meet this need for me - especially in this moment?
2. Is this infringement logical to me? Is my logic understandable or agreeable to them? Is it reasonable for them to understand or agree with me about this - especially in this moment?
3. Is my desire/expectation ethical to me? Is it feasible for them to understand or agree with my ethics, values, or beliefs - especially in this moment?

At this point, it is really about feasibility and reasonableness. There is one overarching question that really overrules the three questions above:

In a balanced and emotionally healthy world, does my level of response match the level of the offense?

I can't tell you how often I ask this question and get embarrassed by my own answer - "NO!"

Oftentimes if we step back a little from the situation and take a look at our own mounting emotional response, we can realize that our emotions are rising up past the level of offense, whether it is accidental and intentional. We are just getting unnecessarily butt-hurt. If you fast-forwarded past the event and looked back with 20/20 vision, would you say you overreacted? If a friend was there with you, you could practice accountable relationship stuff and ask what they thought of your response. I do this all the time. Ask them these questions and rate their answers on a 1 (low) to 10 (high) scale.

- Was my response appropriate?
    - Was it too strong (or too weak)?
- Was what they said appropriate
    - Was what they said too strong (or too weak)

When I get too emotionally strong, and I ask these questions, I almost always find out from my friend that there is a gap between what was said (low score) and how I reacted (high score). Therein lies the problem - the gap. Healthy and good Emotional Intelligence takes responsibility to address the gap while not denying or disrespecting your own context, facts, and feelings. With Emotional Intelligence, this is done with calmness, directness, and immediacy.

Here are some more ways you can process each infringement:

- *Needs Infringement:* Ask yourself some feasibility questions. Do I need a nap or a snack? It will not likely be possible to sprawl out on the floor right then and there for a power nap or ask them if they have a granola bar in their pocket while you are rolling your eyes or flaring your nostrils at them. It's likely not appropriate, especially for men, to stop and ask for a hug if you are feeling insecure or isolated in the moment. Although, you could manage the moment better by telling yourself that as soon as you get a chance, you can rectify the problem in a bit, but that in the current moment you are becoming emotional because of a compounded problem of an unmet need. So be honest in the moment. Tell them you are feeling emotional and should stick a tack in the discussion and come back to it later. Tell them you are a little frazzled or a little tired or a little grumpy or a little "off" in the moment. Be sure to come back to it. Don't be a coward and avoid them and the issue when you cross paths the next time.

- *Intellectual Infringement:* Ask yourself some feasibility questions. Is it logical for me to expect this person to agree with me or to know what I have come to know? If the person doesn't have the benefit of your knowledge, however you got it, it is not logical for you to expect them to know or agree with you. Don't ask this so you can feel really smart and be really condescending. The answer to this question oftentimes is "No". After that remind yourself that you are the one being emotional and that you are the one trying to manage your emotions. Then remember that logic and emotion seldom mix well. After that try to close the gap by explaining some of your logic/knowledge to them. Keep in mind that they may not agree or be interested, but you are trying to explain why you "feel" so strongly about it. Seek to explain the knowledge gap rather than being emotionally offended or butt-hurt.

- *Belief/Value/Conviction Infringement:* Ask yourself some feasibility questions. How likely is it that my friend will/can embrace my beliefs, values, or convictions on this subject - especially in the moment? Can we agree to disagree and smile while we do it? Remember that it is likely that you acquired the belief, value or conviction over a course of time, after needs were met and knowledge was gained. Coming to the same page about beliefs, values or conviction may require many conversations with each other - and agreement may or may not be reached. Perhaps a deeper and more meaningful friendship can be reached! Releasing the person from their accidental, intentional or purposeful offense because of differing values, beliefs, or convictions can be freeing and emotionally healthy.

TRAUMA DRAMA

Just this morning, I was talking to my brother whom I have referred to many times in this book. A part of our conversation was about our traumatic upbringing that was so chaotic and unpredictable. At any moment things could change dramatically and traumatically. The emotional parts of our brains learned to always be on guard for the next upheaval. We got so used to drama that we didn't know we lived in a constant state of it.

As I learned about Emotional Intelligence, I was able to begin to retrain the emotional centers of my mental processing and manage my moments much better. Even more recently I have learned that trauma has its own domain in our emotional and mental processing. Trauma runs deep! And trauma has really fast currents that take us places we don't want to go. Trauma creates triggers whether we want to admit it or not.

At the beginning of this chapter, I shared with you how I didn't really like being labeled a trauma guy by one of my gritty friends. He was referring to a conflict with another mutual friend. Since that time my friend and I have worked through the conflict. But I had to admit some things about my lack of emotional intelligence from that incident. I had a level 8-9 reaction to a level 3-4 offense. And I reacted really strongly. I was trained to act strongly. Acting strongly was the only way I could survive in the family I grew up in. Even though my friend and I worked through it, my strong response did some damage and it almost fractured the relationship beyond repair. My friend and I talked it through and we are on great terms again. But I was a bit haunted by my strong reaction. Why did I go to such a high level of reaction so easily?

I had to admit to myself, and to a couple of my gritty friends, that there is part of me - the trauma-affected part of me - that thrives on drama. I could say it is not my fault because my brain and my neuro-processors are used to it - maybe even addicted to it (there is science behind that too). But that would be blaming my past and not taking responsibility for my present or my future. My response-ability is my responsibility.

A truth about me is there is a part of me that creates deep drama from shallow incidents. It is how I have learned to figure out what to do next.

I am going to tell you something that I do that I am not proud of and that might make you toss this book in the trash. I start every morning of the day sitting in my backyard jacuzzi with coffee and thinking and talking to Jesus (that's not the part that should make you throw this book in the trash - after all you are almost done reading the book at this point...) Here's the embarrassing part: there are some mornings that I ask myself a trauma-induced, paranoid, drama-king question. What am I upset about today? Who am I mad at?" An otherwise peaceful start of a great day gets interrupted with me trying to conjure up unhappiness and drama.

That is NOT Emotional Intelligence - that is self-induced emotional drama that verges on emotional entrapment. Who wants to live like that? Not me! And I don't think my friends do either.

Just like I am determined to never bite my fingernails again, I am determined to stop manufacturing drama from my trauma. I am determined to not live in drama but live in peace and harmony with my God, myself and my community. I am doing this by increasing my Emotional intelligence and telling a few gritty men about it so they can hold me accountable and help me grow through it.

Maybe you are a drama manufacturer like me. Stop it. Maybe you are the typical male - not fully understanding emotions. Stop it. Maybe you get too angry too easily. Stop it. Whatever the case, all of us can afford more Emotional Intelligence. Commit to developing your Emotional Intelligence and do it with some gritty friends.

DISCUSSION QUESTIONS

1. How much of a drama king are you? How much of an emotional pauper are you?
2. How do you feel when someone asks you how you feel? Do you use feeling words or fact words?

3. How easily are you triggered into anger or some other irrational emotion? How hard is it for you to control those surges?
4. Are you triggered most by needs infringements, intellectual infringements or beliefs/values/convictions infringements?
5. On a 1 (low) to 10 (high) scale, how would your friends rate your Emotional Intelligence? How could you increase it?

8
Gritty Longevity

The best mirror is an old friend.
— George Herbert - Early 17th Century Poet/Clergyman

SKELETON FRIENDS

A few years ago, a fellow partner in ministry was reviewing her many years in church ministry. She said that as she thought back over the years of church ministry, it was like a life pathway that was strewn with the skeletons of former relationships. Friend after friend was gone - for a variety of reasons: - some negative, some neutral, some circumstantial, some problematic, some missed and some not. Granted, she and her husband were ending one ministry assignment without knowing what the next one would be. She was lamenting over lost friendships while grappling with all the energy that starting new ones was going to take once they landed somewhere new.

It bothered me a lot because it was my wife. I tried to encourage her and take the blame. It was because of my job - as a pastor. And it was my desire to have continual impact and my impact had reached a ceiling in my current setting. I was looking for a new job at a different church. Here we were again - about to lose meaningful and gritty relationships - again.

The big question she was asking was: "Why were there so many dead friendships in our life?" The reasons are many. It reminded me of some scripture in the Old Testament of Ezekiel[72] where God's Spirit talks to Ezekiel in a vision. He shows him a dry valley with skeletons strewn across the desert. But the skeletons were about to get a reboot - he was about to reanimate them into thriving people again. God was going to breathe life into dry skeletons. I was really hoping it would happen that way for us at whatever new church we ended up.

TRANSIENT FRIENDSHIPS

Most people have their own bone piles strewn along the pathway of friendships in their lives. Why is this so? Why are friendships fleeting and fleeing? Why do friendships die while people are still alive?

There are so many practical answers for those questions. People relocate because of wanderlust or maybe because of career changes and promotions. Then distance turns into time and both time and distance separate friends from each other longer than they ever thought would happen. People have kids and hobbies that don't have much crossover in time, interest or activity, so their paths don't cross until months turn into years

---

[72] Ezekiel 37:1-4

without seeing each other. Friends get offended and hurt and instead of tending to it through trust and communication, they let the relationship start to bleed out until it gets a little anemic and infected. When it does finally heal up, all that is left is the scar of a failed friendship that was once important, meaningful and gritty.

There are other sociological reasons for Skeleton Friendships.

Social Promiscuity - Many skeleton relationships, especially among young adults, come at the hands of "social promiscuity". One study found that younger men and women are becoming socially promiscuous – making lots of friends and social contacts up to the age of 25. After that they started losing friendships rapidly, and the dead friendships keep stacking up until the age of retirement.[73] At that point, people begin to decide what is most important – and valuable – in their life. It turns out the "what" is actually the "who". It is friends. About the time people retire, they begin to make a greater effort to hold on to friendships. That seems a little late. It also seems like that leaves a lot of friendship skeletons in the valley of life.

Adhocracy - Another reason for diminishing friendships is that too many friendships these days are "ad hoc". Ad Hoc relationships are transactional and replaceable. In his book "Future Shock"[74], Alvin Toffler predicted the coming of transience in many areas of life and society. Toffler said that transience springs from the increasing temporariness in everyday life. He predicted that transience would have a high impact on the world's economy, technology and especially friendships. If people, governments, and jobs become temporary, then

---

[73] Senthilingam, Meera. This is the age when you start losing friends. CNN Health. June 6, 2016. https://www.cnn.com/2016/06/06/health/losing-friends-mid-twenties/index.html

[74] Toffler, Alvin. Future Shock. Random House, Inc. 0-394-42586-3. 1970.

relationships would not be immune. And this book was hauntily enough written in 1970.

Toffler refers to this social phenomena as adhocracy - a social circle made up of ad hoc (temporary) members that use each other for seasons and reasons but are not in it for the long haul. These types of friendships are transactional because they are more like a transaction. Once the relationship has met a need in the person's life, the relationship is ended and replaced with a relationship that helps meet the next transactional goal, whether that is a new job, a new house, a new social standing, etc. As a result, friendships not only lack longevity, they also lack meaning.

Malienation - As men age, it is the all too common misfortune that bellies increase, but friendships don't, As economies ebb and flow in and out of recession, male friendships are on a consistent downward recession. Studies consistently show that men are lonelier than women and that men are more lonely now than they ever have been. A 2022 article from the New York post reported:

> When looking at both men and women, just 59% of Americans can identify one person as their "best friend," down from 77% in 1990, the poll found.
>
> Nearly 1 in 5 American men admit to not having a single close friend, according to the results of the American Perspectives Survey, conducted by the Survey Center on American Life.
>
> The number of American men without a close friend has jumped five times since 1995, from 3% to 15%, according to the findings, while those claiming to have

at least six close friends have plunged by half, from 55% to 27%.[75]

Malienation is a made up word[76], but it is a real phenomena. Malienation is more than loneliness. It is an alienation from what was once experienced among men when they were boys. It's more like an estrangement from the male brotherhood that was bound together by adventure and vulnerability.

It's the estrangement from an embodied and vulnerable brotherhood. A built-in understanding of what it's like to joust with fallen tree branches, evade bullies, build forts, heave yourself atop a pileup of bodies to test the threshold between play and aggression, share secrets, and wipe away your snot but leave your tears. Malienation is mourning this love, this synergy between emotionality and physicality.[77]

I was reminded of this estrangement only a few weeks ago. I had the pleasure of attending my fortieth high school reunion. I loved it! I got to see people I hadn't seen in forty years - and we all looked the same (as if)! I actually couldn't believe that after forty years, while we may not have looked the same, we really were close to the same. Even though we had been shaped by life's blessings, successes, failures and disappointments, I recognized the laughs, smiles, voices and mannerisms of these people that had made much more of an impact on my life than I had realized.

One afternoon of that weekend, I took my brother, who was tagging along (just like the growing up years...) to one of our old adventure haunts - a treehouse down by an isolated

---

[75] Diaz, Adriana. Men suffer 'friendship recession' as 15% are without a single close pal. July 7, 2021. https://nypost.com/2021/07/07/friendship-recession-15-of-men-are-without-a-close-pal/.

[76] Stone, Jet, Ph.D. Why Men Need to Prioritize, and Celebrate, Their Friendships: It should be OK for men to miss men. February 8, 2022. https://www.psychologytoday.com/us/blog/the-souls-men/202202/why-men-need-prioritize-and-celebrate-their-friendships

[77] Ibid

creek not far from our neighborhood. Our neighborhood was isolated, so it really was our creek - our private playground. Our friends came to our treehouse by our invitation. Our treehouse only had a floor - no walls. We never finished it, but it turned out to be an advantage because we could see if anyone dared tread close to our private enclave. We read books there - snuck cigarettes there, avoided our parents there. It was a grand place!

I was there a few years ago. The remnants of the treehouse were still there! The wood 2X4 planks of the floor were still intact. My brother and I hadn't been there together for more than the 40 years that had passed since I had graduated from high school. As we made our way to the tree, I was aghast and confused. The tree wasn't there anymore. As I foraged around, I found a fallen tree in the area where our tree had been. I was certain it was our tree. I was determined to find remnants of our tree house in the chaotic stack of freshly rotting wood. And I did! I have even included picture proof for you. Can you see the head of a nail and 2 nails sticking into the branch?!

That tree house was more than a tree house. The adventures my brother and I had had with our friends there were so important and pivotal. Since then we really did become victims of malienation. We stopped having adventures together. We stopped being vulnerable with each other. And I have already told you, that sixteen years slipped by with almost no contact with my brother. We made up for some of it that weekend!

Here's another story of intentionally smashing the gradual effects of malienation:

> The Tuesday before every Thanksgiving, Aaron Karo and Matt Ritter, both 43, go out to dinner with a group of seven men whom they befriended as second graders in Plainview, N.Y.
>
> At the dinner, one of the friends wins the Man of the Year prize — a silly accolade the group concocted as an excuse to reconnect. They eat and they laugh, and the winner leaves with his name engraved on a cartoonishly large silver cup.
>
> "It's not really about the trophy," said Mr. Karo, who co-hosts a podcast with Mr. Ritter called "Man of the Year," which explores adult friendship. "It's about the traditions that keep us together." The friends jockey for the prize in a running group text, where they share memes and talk a bit of trash but also keep up with one another.[78]

How can men have relationships like that? How can men have gritty relationships that stand the test of time? How can men have relationships with staying power?

---

[78] Pearson, Catherine. Why Is It So Hard For Men To Make Close Friends? American men are stuck in a "friendship recession." Here's how to climb out. November 28, 2022. https://www.nytimes.com/2022/11/28/well/family/male-friendship-loneliness.html

FRIENDSHIP TOUGHNESS

Mental Toughness is a popular self-awareness and self-management skill that is gaining popularity. It is the ability to confront and overcome challenges, adversity, or setbacks with resilience and determination. Mental toughness helps us become our best self in the face of hard circumstances. James Clear, a New York Times bestselling author, talks about mental toughness exhibited by some of the 1300 cadets who start West Point Academy each summer.

It wasn't strength or smarts or leadership potential that accurately predicted whether or not a cadet would finish Beast Barracks. Instead, it was grit — the perseverance and passion to achieve long-term goals — that made the difference.[79]

Consistency: Clear goes on to describe one of the more prominent aspects of mental toughness exhibited in various vocations:

Mentally tough athletes are more consistent than others. They don't miss workouts. They don't miss assignments. They always have their teammates back.

Mentally tough leaders are more consistent than their peers. They have a clear goal that they work towards each day. They don't let short-term profits, negative feedback, or hectic schedules prevent them from continuing the march towards their vision. They make a habit of building up the people around them — not just once, but over and over and over again.

Mentally tough artists, writers, and employees deliver on a more consistent basis than most. They work on a schedule, not just when they feel motivated. They approach their work like a pro, not an amateur. They do the most important thing first and don't shirk responsibilities.[80]

---

[79] Clear, James. The Science of Developing Mental Toughness in Your Health, Work, and Life. https://jamesclear.com/mental-toughness. Downloaded August 28, 2023.
[80] Ibid

Did you see what one of the key elements of mental toughness? It was consistency. What if we applied some of Clear's consistency factors of mental toughness to friendships to make them more gritty?

- Mentally tough friends are more consistent than other friends. They don't miss time with friends. They keep their friends a priority by making time with their friends a priority.
- Mentally tough friends go beyond spending time with each other. Rather than missing things about their friends, mentally tough friends notice things about their friends. They consistently pay attention to their life events, their moods, and to their highs and lows.
- Mentally tough friends have their friend's back. They keep guard while they stand in each other's corner. They block things from coming to them and when they can't block them, they whisper in their ear (or shout to their face) to warn them about what is coming - or might be coming.
- Mentally tough friends show up when they say they are going to, and even when they didn't say they were going to.

Consistency is key for mentally tough friendships. One of the biggest killers of gritty friendships is neglect and inconsistency. Letting a friend down lets more than air out of the circumstance, it deflates the friendship.

I had a friend a while back who was pretty consistently inconsistent. He regularly let me down in ways that mattered. When we were together it was a lot of fun. Our conversations were deep and elicited spiritual and emotional growth in both of us. The problem was when we would get going on things, he would start to flake out on getting together, usually because he wasn't following through well or he was retreating into bad habits brought on by trauma and insecurity. He also pulled out of some commitments that left me hanging emotionally and even financially. I ended up doing some significant things all alone that we were going to do together. It did add up and took its toll on our friendship. It definitely became less gritty.

Here are some easy, but tough questions and thoughts to ask yourself to help figure out if you are a mentally tough friend.

- Are you an Amateur or An Expert: Would you consider yourself a friendship amateur? How would your closest friends answer that question if they knew you wouldn't see the answer? What would it take to become a friendship pro with a couple of friends?
- Are you a Disneyland Friend or Gritty Friend? On a scale of 1 (low) to 10 (high), how consistent are you as a friend - not just in showing up for the fun things, but the unplanned, unfun things that can derail a guy if he has to go through it alone and derail a friendship for the same reason? If you are brave, ask your closest friends to give you an honest number and some reasons why.
- Define what friendship toughness means for you. Define what you think it means to your closest friends? Tell them what you think it means to them and ask them if you have it right. And then tell them what friendship toughness means to you.
- Friendship toughness is built through small wins. We don't get it right all the time. All of us suffer from what I call breaking the friendship L.A.W. from time to time. We break the friendship L.A.W. when we are too Lazy, too Apathetic or too Weary in our friendships. All

three are remedial - which means we can do something about each - all three have a remedy. We can quit being friendship lazy by getting off our lazy friendship butts and check in with a friend with a text message or hang out with them in person. We can develop some passion for our friends and their lives and care about what really matters to them, or what could matter to them if they stepped up to it. Or we can take a nap so we can be awake and aware of what is going on in our friends' lives rather than be clueless.

As you can see, friendship toughness is about your friendship habits. But what is our motivation to be tough friends? Why do we have friends in the first place? One simple reason is that we are social creatures. We are created to be in relationships - the one we have with ourselves and the one we have with each other.

Even though I am an extrovert, I really enjoy time alone. For years I have made it a habit to take quarterly spiritual retreats. Usually I go camping. As a pastor, it helps me connect with God and helps me detox from the rigors of church work so I can return refreshed and ready to jump into my work and my relationships with new zeal and fervor. As valuable as that habit is, I have learned that I am good for 48 hours at the maximum - 36 hours are just about enough. If I am alone longer than that, two things happen. I get lonely and I get selfish. I want to get home to see my wife, my dogs and my friends. Sometimes the urge to go home is so strong that I pack up in the midday of the second day because I want to get home and sleep in a bed with my wife instead of in a tent by myself. But if I stay away too long, when I do return, I am more grumpy and less refreshed - which defeats the purpose of the personal spiritual retreat in the first place. I have spent so much time thinking to myself, talking to myself and doing everything I want to do in the moment that I want to do it. I end up being impatient as I reassimilate into selflessness from a state of selfishness. I remember years ago when I first made this a practice, the church secretary said to me, "I thought you were supposed to come back from these retreats nicer not meaner." Simply put, we are better together.

Seeking input from more than yourself is also a good reason to have friendship toughness. Another self-management habit I have learned to maintain is talking out my thoughts with friends. This practice keeps me mentally and spiritually happier and articulate. I am deeply introspective - maybe even to a fault. I really tend to overprocess things - whether they be relationships, problems or strategies. My overthinking starts circling slowly until it becomes like a vortex that sucks all of my thinking and reasoning and emotion into it. When this is positive thinking, it works out well. When it is negative thinking, it is dangerous. I have learned that when I enter into the overthinking vortex, if I don't talk to someone with skin, then I end up making bad decisions that hurt me, the situation and people I care about. I have a policy, that when I start circling the over-processing vortex, I have to meet up with one of my gritty friends and tell them what I have been thinking about - or overthinking about... This interrupts the vortex thinking. It also forces me to become articulate about the things I have been vortexing about. And because I am sharing it with a gritty friend, I know they will be honest about my thinking and especially about my conclusions. Then I can move forward.

There are some other more scientific reasons why friendship habits are important. People with gritty friends are more satisfied with their lives and less likely to suffer from depression.[81] They're also less likely to die from all causes, including heart problems and a range of chronic diseases.[82] Friendship toughness actually protects us by changing the way we respond to stress. When I enter the over-processing vortex, chances are my blood pressure increases. Studies show talking with a gritty friend has the opposite effect. Blood pressure decreases when people talk to a supportive friend rather than a friend they aren't very close to.[83] The same thing happens when we have a friend by our side while completing a tough task.[84] One study showed people even judged a hill to be less steep when they were accompanied by a friend.[85]

Friendship Toughness is really about consistency. Friendship toughness is all about making gritty relationships a habit. This means that in order for a friendship to be meaningful, it needs to be nurtured.

In the masculine realm, nurturing isn't really a man's native tongue - not his go-to behavior. Nurturing is really about intentional growth and encouragement.[86] Nurturing relationships are win/win relationships. An easy way to nurture a friendship is to help your friend achieve some of their wins. Help remove obstacles. Most of the time obstacles can be removed simply by talking through the obstacles so your friend can see their way through to the other side. For me that is one of the biggest ways to overcome an obstacle. When something blocks my way, I quickly become the worst version of myself. Talking with

---

[81] Choi, K. W., et al., The American Journal of Psychiatry, Vol. 177, No. 10, 2020
[82] Holt-Lunstad, J., et al., PLOS Medicine, Vol. 7, No. 7, 2010; Steptoe, A., et al., PNAS, Vol. 110, No. 15, 2013.
[83] Holt-Lunstad, J., et al., Annals of Behavioral Medicine, Vol. 33, No. 3, 2007.
[84] Kamarck, T. W., et al., Psychosomatic Medicine, Vol. 52, No. 1, 1990.
[85] Schnall, S., et al., Journal of Experimental Social Psychology, Vol. 44, No. 5, 2008.
[86] Oxford Dictionary. https://www.oed.com/search/dictionary/?scope=Entries&q=Nurture

a friend about the factors blocking my way forward is really important. If I do this, it usually prevents me from making a bad decision or blurting out a damaging comment that is hard to take back. Nurturing isn't all about hugs and fuzzy words.

Men don't want to appear emotionally needy. A certain amount of machismo goes into [male] friendships.[87]

Men can be nurturing and masculine at the same time. Nurturing a male friendship is more about reaching each others' important relationship goals and being a positive contributor to your friend and his future. This is very masculine since men love to have goals and are solution-based.

Nurturing friendship is important because when we are alone we are lesser than we are made to be. When we are alone, we migrate toward the easier and worse habits that tear down a life more than they build a life up. Friendship toughness comes down to this. Friendships have to be nurtured or they become run of the mill, shallow friendships that have very little meaning or that fade away and evaporate into memories that don't shape our futures anymore.

SEASONAL STAYING POWER

Does this notion of nurturing friendships with staying power mean that you are stuck with your current friendships for the rest of your life, and if you don't nurture them, you're a failed friend?

Maybe.

---

[87] Diago, Mike. The Real Reason Men Struggle With Friendship: Making friends is something we learn how to do when we're still in diapers. So why are grown men so bad at it? Fatherly. May 23, 2023. https://www.fatherly.com/health/male-friendship-dr-greif

The fact of friendships is that things in life change: our geography changes when we move, life-focus changes when we gain a new passion or calling, lifestyle changes when we get a new girlfriend or a raise, or priorities shift when we start raising kids, and these all have an effect on friendships.

And then you end up with dead relationships along the way. But some friendships aren't really dead. They are just redefined, realigned, refocused or dormant - for a season.

One of the best examples of friendships with staying power is the biblical friendship of David and Jonathan. Their friendship was deep, and complicated. Jonathan's dad, Saul, was the first King of Israel. After he had become King (and he didn't even want the job at first), David became a member of his "court" as a musician. But there was a whole lot more to David than musical aptitude. He was a skilled shepherd, he was smart and wise, and was a super effective and efficient soldier, and quickly became noticed for those things and became the next King-apparent to replace Saul at some point in the future.

In the middle of all of that, David married Saul's daughter and became best friends with his son. King Saul got really jealous and threatened, even though David was really humble and in no way aspirational for Saul's job. Saul got really bitter and vengeful. His vehemence against David grew so strong that he gathered a brigade to hunt him down to kill him.

During this time, Jonathan and David somehow maintained their very close friendship. It was Jonathan who warned David that his own father was out to kill him and helped him stay hidden and get away from an approaching onslaught. Early in the relationship, they made a covenant with each other to have staying power. In the eighteenth chapter of the book of

1 Samuel, it says "the soul of Jonathan was knit to the soul of David, and Jonathan loved him as his own soul".[88]

This seems even more amazing because Jonathan was a political and war specimen himself, and because of that and because he was the son of the current King, he would likely have become the next king if David hadn't come along. But instead of acting like his father, he made a commitment to David as a gritty friend and continually followed through with the commitment. Later on, Jonathan, who was loyal to his country, Israel, and his father while staying committed to David, was killed in battle in the same battle his father killed himself to avoid enemy capture. David, also showing staying power to Jonathan and remaining loyal to King Saul, retrieved both of their bodies from the enemy occupied territory and honored them with a proper burial. He said really nice and honorable things about King Saul, the murderous conspirator. He also made a notable speech for Jonathan. Here is one sentence from that speech about their relationship:

> Jonathan lies slain on your high places. I am distressed for you, my brother Jonathan; very pleasant have you been to me; your love to me was extraordinary, surpassing the love of women.[89]

They were close and they were really committed to each other as gritty friends. That couldn't have been an easy thing to manage for Jonathan when his own father was carrying out a bitter and orchestrated death vendetta on his best friend. I am pretty sure they had to have an agreement to never bring up David at family dinners. Not only that, but David and Jonathan

---

[88] English Standard Version of the Bible
[89] 1 Samuel 1:26. English Standard Version of the Holy Bible.

had extended seasons where they couldn't be around each other because David was fleeing for his life, and Jonathan was fighting for his country alongside his father. In his eulogy for Saul and Jonathan, David also said this about their friendship:

> Saul and Jonathan, beloved and lovely! In life and in death they were not divided; they were swifter than eagles; they were stronger than lions.[90]

In this same lament, he described the gritty relationship this father and son had together. They were totally united, swifter than eagles and stronger than lions. And then he describes his feelings for both of them as beloved and lovely. This is a really good definition for all gritty relationships. Chances are pretty slim that most male friendships don't use "beloved' and "lovely" to describe their meaningful and gritty relationships. But they should. The Hebrew words bring even more meaning. Beloved means to have emotional affection for your friend and lovely means that your friend brings you delight and joy.

David and Jonathan's relationship had highs and lows like our friendships do. Their friendship had seasons of isolation - in fact some of David's most intimate, vulnerable, and dark Psalms were written when he was isolated from people, including Jonathan - which also tell us what happens when we are deprived of our gritty relationships.

The point is this. Their friendship was maintained even though it had seasons when they were totally aligned and present with each other or even when they were pursuing opposite agendas and not spending any time together.

---

[90] 2 Samuel 1:23. English Standard Version of the Holy Bible.

We, too, can have seasons of alignment and proximity and seasons of alienation and vacancy. But the basic tenet and fabric of our friendships can maintain a gritty core so when we do enter into a new season of closeness and connection, we return to the depth and poignancy a gritty friendship provides.

This chapter has been the toughest of chapters to write. I have had to be honest about my own track record, and the trail of skeleton friendships my wife referred to at the beginning of this chapter.

There is one relationship that has been haunting me while I write this chapter because at one point, it was really gritty and important. It isn't anymore. In fact, I have been avoiding reaching out to this friend to see if we can reconcile the distance - for two years. In all candor, I was not brave enough and didn't want to be inconvenienced by the work it would take to reconcile and I didn't want to risk him declining an invitation for reconciliation.

Every time I'd sit down to work on this chapter, I would tell you how to have a gritty relationship for the long haul and think about not being able to do that with this guy. I am happy to say that in spite of my hesitation, by God's grace, and my friend's initiative, he actually reached out to me a couple of weeks ago. When he is back in town in a couple of months we are going to have coffee. We will see if we get to be gritty again.

GONE, BUT STILL PRESENT

Time does not diminish friend-
ship, nor does separation.

- Tennessee Ernie Ford - 20th century
singer and television host

A year and a half ago, a past friend reached out to me in a social media message. I was really surprised - by a picture message of a message written by me from more than 20 years ago. Here is what I saw in my own handwriting:

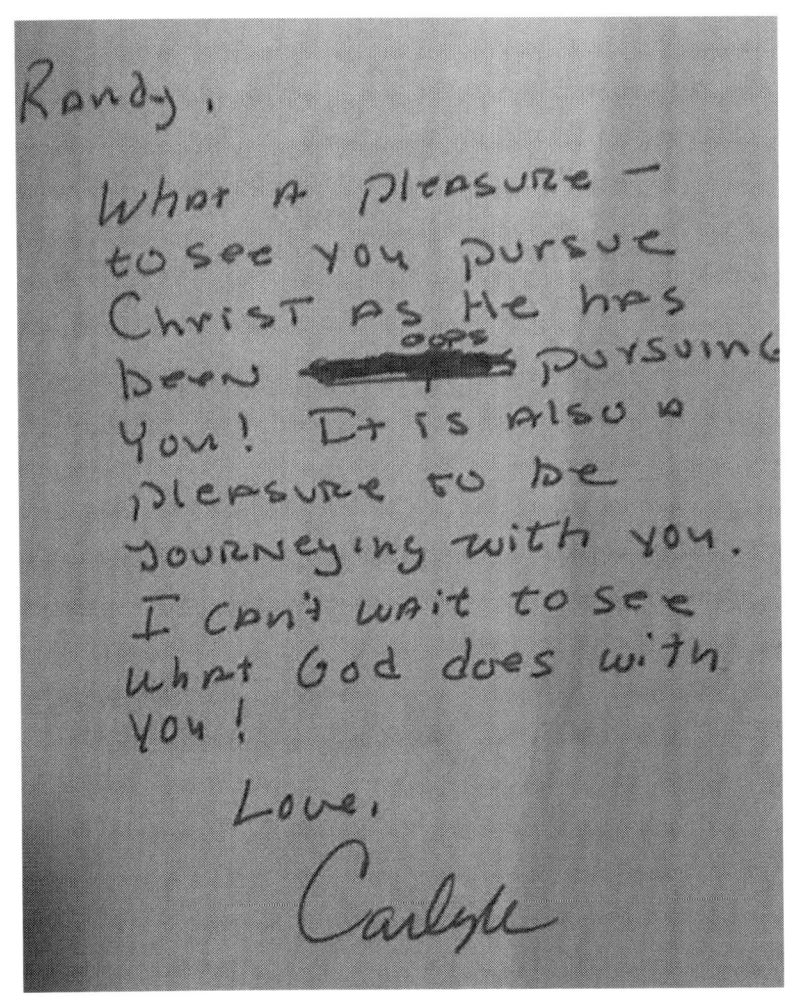

> Randy,
>
> What a pleasure - to see you pursue Christ as He has been ~~oops~~ pursuing you! It is also a pleasure to be journeying with you. I can't wait to see what God does with you!
>
> Love,
> Carlyle

When I saw the note in my writing, it seemed gritty, but also spooky because I couldn't remember who I had written it to. He followed it with a message from him and we had a quick instant message conversation:

That was in 2002. I figured it was high time for an update. I'd love to see you, buddy. I am back in the valley after being gone for almost 20 years. That was one of the reasons I've been hunting you down. You said you can't wait to see what Jesus does with me. Well, guess what? After all these years, he finally got my attention and I think I have a calling. Hope you are well Carlyle (except he misspelled my name which I was willing to forgive since I was struggling to remember details of our friendship in that moment). I hope you remember me. I'm one of hundreds of people you baptized out here on the east side of town.

I wrote the note and gave it to him at his baptism. I started to rifle through my memories and started to remember some things about him. So I messaged back.

Hey! Yeah. It took me a few seconds to think back. But I do remember you, where you lived and stuff like that. But I can't remember what happened to you.

Jog my memory.

We filled in a few more blanks with a few more instant messages. He said he was going to come to my church on the other side of town from him - which for him was almost half-way to Los Angeles. He did show up and I was so taken aback by his greeting to me. There were no words. He simply started sobbing from his belly. He walked up to me and put his head onto my shoulder as we hugged in the lobby of my church. He was beside himself by seeing me again. And I felt guilty, because I still wasn't remembering many details about the gritty and intimate conversations we had that he was telling me about.

That is a gritty relationship that has a season that made a difference in a man's life - and the memory of it made a difference in my life too. That is the type of relationships men need to have - even if we do have seasons of connection and disconnection. If it is gritty, it stands that test of time and separation and has staying power!

DISCUSSION QUESTIONS

1. How big is the trail of skeleton friendships in your life? What are some of the reasons they are dead?
2. What friendships did you think were dead that actually came back to life? How did that occur? Who initiated it?
3. Are you a mentally tough friend? How do you know that to be true or untrue?
4. Can you think of friendships that were gritty at one point, but aren't anymore? Can you reach out to that old friend and tell them how much their friendship meant to you back then? If you are hesitant, why?
5. Who is already in your life who is or could be a gritty friend with friendship toughness and staying power? What are you willing and able to do to make it that way?

9
Gritty Legacy

To leave the world a bit better, whether by a healthy child, a garden patch, or a redeemed social condition; to know that even one life has breathed easier because you have lived - that is to have succeeded.
— Ralph Waldo Emerson - 19th Century American essayist, lecturer, philosopher, abolitionist, and poet

But even if I am being poured out like a drink offering on the sacrifice and service coming from your faith, I am glad and rejoice with all of you.
— The Apostle Paul from the letter to the Philippian Church.

DEATHBED PANIC

The look in his eye was not one I see often and not one I ever enjoy seeing. It was a look of profound fear - not fear of an IRS audit or that you have cancer. It was the juxtaposition of certainty commingling with uncertainty. It was the look that precedes imminent and certain death. It was the look of panic - about his future and his legacy.

The man I was looking at was in a hospital bed and was grappling with his last days - literally. A few weeks earlier life was pretty normal. He was going about his life business as a retired man with a wife who loved him, dogs that loved him and some grandkids and kids who loved him. But then, out of the blue, he started having some stomach problems. He was diagnosed with bad cancer that was inoperable and invasive. Things changed really quickly.

I knew his wife from church. She was a stalwart member of my congregation. She attended almost every Sunday - with her girlfriends but never her husband. He had graced us with his presence at a couple of special occasions, like Christmas Eve and Easter. He was never antagonistic to her faith and hope in Jesus, just not interested.

He was interested the day I came to see him. He was asking himself the two biggest questions all of us ask sooner or later:

- What is going to happen to me after I die?
- After I am gone, will my life matter?

He asked me to come and visit with him. I was honored to do so. But that look in his eye...it was profound. It still both haunts me, and it still gives me hope. We had a good conversation about life, death and eternity. He did some business with God that day. I think he did some business with how his life mattered that day too. I think he got some answers to those two super-important questions - and just in time. He died only a few days later.

As important as the conversation was for him, I wonder if he was disappointed that he hadn't sought out answers to those two big questions earlier. I wonder if he was disappointed that he hadn't lived out the answer yet.

At their deathbed, almost all of the stories we hear about are regrets about legacy, not money or possessions. Men and women alike ponder their legacy by pondering their influence on the people around them. They want to know their ripple won't just cease. They want to know their breaths didn't just vaporize. They want to know their souls mattered - to other souls.

All of us leave something behind. Sometimes it is just a wet, soiled towel on the locker room floor of life.

CASTING OFF GOOD SEED

In his last message, Sir Robert Baden-Powell, the founder of the Boy Scouts, told scouts to "try to leave the world a little better than you found it". His legacy-making phrase and life message caught on. After an inspiring meeting with Sir Baden-Powell, Juliette Gordon Low established the Girl Scouts later that year and adopted his mantra of leaving the world a better place. Baden-Powell was passing on a legacy that was passed to him. He got the inspiration of his phrase from Ralph Waldo Emerson, a 19th century poet who often wrote about nature around us and the nature inside of us.

> To leave the world a bit better, whether by a healthy child, a garden patch, or a redeemed social condition; to know that even one life has breathed easier because you have lived - that is to have succeeded.

The Boy Scouts adopted the mantra back in the day, especially when it came to camping. But over the years it got condensed to "leave no trace".[91] For campsites that is a good policy. For a life, not so much!

We want to leave a trace. Really, don't we want to leave more than a trace? Don't we want to leave more than just evidence that we lived? Don't we all want to leave evidence that we mattered and that we made a difference? This legacy-quest is intrinsic in humans and maybe even more so in men and can be traced back to some basic biological differences between men and women. Both men and women leave a legacy. For women, it is much more verifiable and quantifiable - it can be both seen and counted. For men, we are just more expendable than women. It has always been so.

Men are more attracted to risk and have greater physical strength than women, so they have always been slotted for society's dirtiest and most dangerous jobs. Like hunting and war.

In World War I, there were 9.7 million, almost exclusively male, military deaths. The number boggles the mind: 10 million men went off to war and never came home. Enormously tragic, but on a certain level we accept it; it is inconceivable to imagine 10 million women being sent to the slaughter instead. 6,025 American service members have died in the Iraq and Afghanistan wars. Only 2% of the fallen were women. Men made up 93% of the 6,000 on-the-job deaths last year.[92]

When life is tragically at stake, things like wealth and race play second fiddle to women.

When the Titanic sunk, the survival rate for rich, first class men (34%) was lower than that of the poor, third-class women (46%).[93]

---

[91] https://www.scouting.org/outdoor-programs/leave-no-trace/. Visited site September 20, 2023.
[92] The Five Switches of Manliness: Legacy. https://www.artofmanliness.com/character/behavior/the-5-switches-of-manliness-legacy/. June 13, 2011. Last updated: September 25, 2021. Visited site September 10, 2023.
[93] Ibid

When you hear tragic stories of tragic human death, how is it usually reported? Deaths of women and children are always emphasized more and differently than those of men. The death of a woman has more of a bite to society than the death of a man. When a woman dies giving her life for someone or something other than herself, it is a travesty. When a man does that same thing, it is noble. Men's lives are differently valuable than women's - maybe even less. And that makes legacy differently important for a man.

Let's compare some more legacy logistics. How many men can a woman become pregnant from at one time? One. How many women can a man impregnate? Way more than one at a time. Women's eggs are more valuable than a man's sperm. A man's sperm donation can derive anywhere from $25-100[94]. One batch of ejaculate from a man yields up to 100 million sperm cells.[95] That is .000001 cents for each sperm cell.

A woman's egg is generally worth about $5000.[96] The difference is astronomical. And a woman's legacy is more valuable and definable - as the nurturing force behind every human ever born. But men have a really strong pull for legacy too, but with far less opportunity to leave a legacy - especially if they don't die a tragic, noble and noteworthy death. We want a chance to create a noteworthy legacy too. We want to have a more active role in creation than we do by just our sperm donation. I have a close friend who has a wonderful daughter and enjoys their adult relationship, but is plagued by the haunting suspicion that his daughter's mother really just used him as a sperm donor. Men can have an immortal and significant legacy by

---

[94] https://www.supermoney.com/how-much-do-sperm-donors-make/. September 20, 2023
[95] https://www.webmd.com/infertility-and-reproduction/sperm-and-semen-faq. September 20, 2023
[96] https://www.wsj.com/articles/putting-a-price-on-a-human-egg-1437952456. September 20, 2023.

being noble, present and legacy-producing dads. But can we be legacy-producing friends? I think so.

Since we are talking about DNA, reproduction and legacy, I am going to take us back to some of what I shared in Chapter 2 about masculine image-bearing compared to feminine image-bearing. If you remember I emphasized a key verse in the first Chapter of Genesis.

> "God created man in his own image, in the image of God he created him; male and female he created them" (Genesis 1:27, English Standard Version).

In the beginning of the verse, the word for man is more of a generic term that can be likened to humankind. God created humans and they were created to bear the image of God— to reflect aspects of God in human form and experience. The generic reference is clarified in the last phrase. Humankind is described as male and female. There were some distinctions between the two that exceeds physical, moral, and social attributes. They reach deeper into the DNA of masculinity and femininity - they reach into legacy-making!

I have paraphrased the meaning of these two important words. The word for male is "the remembering one." The word for female is "the surrounding one."[97] The male is the one who remembers things—important, life-giving things - and then gives them away!

As the creation story continued, Adam, the first man, was given instructions for living from God himself and he was left to it. Adam commences the work of living, managing the garden, harvesting fruit, and naming the animals. During that work,

---

[97] The Hebrew word for male is "the one who remembers God." The word for female is "to pierce" or "the one who is pierced."

Adam notices that the animals all have another animal of their kind. For Adam, though, no match was present.

In God's great compassion and provision, he created Eve—the surrounding one. Eve joins Adam in the commencing of human living while maintaining a vibrant and personal relationship with God, each other, and their surroundings. There is no mention of God giving the instructions to Eve. It seems that was left to Adam. It was Adam's job to pass on legacy to Eve - to "remember well". Did he remember well? Did he give his legacy away well? No.

In Chapter One, I presented some PG-13 sex education. I basically equated vision-casting to a man choosing to be erect or flaccid. What man doesn't want to pick the first over the second? In fact, as I try to stay PG-13, does a man ever remember not being able to be erect? When I chatted with a man a few years ago who was going in for a prostate surgery, he told me he most likely would never have an erection again. WHAT?!? There are many things that are masculine and manly, but the ability to not be flaccid is definitely one of them!

In the act of sex, as a man "stands firm and erect," the woman surrounds him. The man offers his masculine self to the female who surrounds him, and great sex ensues. As the man stands erect, he casts off his "seed", and if the odds are with him, his seed will propagate a new human being and biological legacy will begin. But is there more to our legacy than sperm cells?

For men, creating legacy is in our genes. In the creation of human life, men may only "cast" off our seed, while the female does almost all of the heavy lifting needed for life to mature and emerge at childbirth. But both male and female continue to be responsible for the ongoing physical, emotional and spiritual development. The problem is that too often, men "cast off" their responsibility for legacy-building after they "cast off" their seed.

If we return to the creation story and fast-forward to Chapter Three of Genesis, we see this very thing happen. Eve is living the garden life, and confusion enters into paradise. She is tempted by a serpent (the devil), who provokes her to doubt God's goodness. She takes the forbidden fruit, snatches a bite while offering a bite to her husband— who was there with her (Genesis 3:6). Many scholars agree that the presence of Adam was more than him walking up on Eve as she wiped the fruity juice off her face. He was present when she was being tempted to question the vision that Adam had passed on to her. But the enlarged travesty of the situation is that Adam, the one who was supposed to stand firm and erect by remembering vision, didn't. He abstained from taking the initiative in the situation, remained silent and passive. He compromised living for him, his wife, and his offspring.

Inside the confines of friendship, when a man fails to initiate, other men experience great loss. And the failed initiator also fails in legacy-making.

When a man fails to leave a legacy, he does not give anyone anything to remember, let alone to remember well.

So how can a man create legacy?

TEACHING A GROWN MAN TO EAT OYSTERS

When a boy is becoming a man, there are many things to be taught. Eating oysters is one of those things. When I was 20 years old, I learned how to eat oysters. I never ate them again. After hearing what I experienced when I ate them, you'll understand.

I was in my second year of marriage. I was beginning a career that started the trajectory of the life coaching and pastoring I would invest in for the rest of my life. The year before, as I was a night shift custodian at a junior high school, I knew I needed to actively invest in a career that could help me finish college while my wife did the same. I enrolled in a vo-tech data processing program. After I finished, to my suprise, the owner of the school reached out to me and said he saw some things in me that could translate into being an instructor at his school. It took me nano seconds to evaluate if I wanted to exchange cleaning toilets for teaching people about computers. The job went really well. Within the first year, a series of events afforded me the opportunity to run the entire business while the owner moved to Phoenix, Arizona. The night before he left, he took me out to dinner at a local restaurant/bar that overlooked the Boise River. I had heard of this place and even drove by it, but had never been inside. It was moderately fancy.

As we sat down to discuss and review that last of the hand-offs, he ordered oyster shooters for us. I really wanted to evoke confidence not just in me, but in my boss's decision to hand off his business-baby to me. I sat up really straight, was dressed like a businessman in 1980's Boise would dress, leaned forward at the right times and laughed at his jokes even when they weren't funny. The oysters came. I had never had oysters before and the plate really surprised me. Oysters in the whole - raw and slimy. I just acted like I knew what I was doing and took some oysters from their shells, slid them onto my appetizer plate and proceeded to cut them into little pieces. Inside I was so grossed out as the raw oyster guts were mutiliated by my butter knife. I would not be deterred as I talked and laughed and secretly gagged, putting grody, mutilated oysters in my mouth, chewing them before I swallowed them. In my mind I was yelling about how terrible this was and may have actually reconsidered my career choice and returned to cleaning toilets - my boss talking and listening and watching. After I had eaten a couple of oysters (I was really making an effort to be a cool businessman), my boss took an oyster, shell and all from the plate, put it to his mouth, and shot the oyster from the shell into his mouth and swallowed it whole. I looked at him in amazement and embarrassment. We laughed really hard together as I told him everything that was going through my mind as I stomached raw oysters for the first and last time.

This exemplifies two important facets of legacy-making:

Legacy = Intentions + Incidents

This man had been extremely intentional about pouring his legacy into me. He saw my potential. He invited me into a visionary future. He instructed me how to be an instructor. He let me design an entirely new program. He introduced me to the back-office parts of his business. Then he offered me the opportunity to run his business for him while he followed his mid-life crisis crush to Phoenix (I know - I left out the reason he moved earlier...).

He also grabbed an incidental opportunity to teach me how to eat oysters after I had miserably failed. He also grabbed the incidental opportunity of me seeking vocational education to give me a job, a career and teach me important aspects of leadership and management.

As a side note, my wife was thinking of him only a few weeks ago. She looked him up and discovered that he had died only a couple of years ago. I had never got around to looking him up myself to let him know of the impact he had on my life and career. While that bums me out a bit, it does tell us how profound a man's legacy can have even when they don't know it. I wonder if I have some guys running around like that - that think of me and my legacy-making contributions I made to their lives. Do you?

Fortunately for me, this wasn't the only man who engaged intentions and incidents to leave a legacy behind.

My introduction into pastoring as a vocation came about similarly when a pastor friend, who had been pouring himself into me spiritually, incidentally asked me about my career future while we were both attending our church's men's retreat. One thing led to another and he invited me to consider pastoring because he saw some things in me that matched the attributes of a pastor. I am happy to say we did not eat oysters together that weekend! From there, my wife and I contemplated a career change for me - that took several months. When I committed to the change, this pastor and I developed a mentoring plan that eventually led to us starting a new church together - my first official pastorate.

There are some easy methods to create intentional and incidental legacy:

Recognize Your Expertise - A few years ago, I was finishing up my doctoral work. My advisor set a lunch appointment with me. As we discussed my dissertation and some other aspects of finishing up my degree, he shifted the subject. He looked me in the eye and told me it was time I realized my areas of expertise and to intentionally offer it to those people younger than me and those farther back on the pathway of effective leadership, theology and pastoring. He said my experience had made some practical impact in my industry (church and ministry), but now it was time to take my almost 30 years of experience and the education of several degrees and hand all of that off on purpose. It was the next logical, respectable, expected step.

I had to come to terms with two truths: 1. I did have things that others would likely enjoy and benefit from knowing; 2. I was entering the latter parts of my career. Both were pretty sobering. The talk impacted me and I began to intentionally, and now maybe even obsessively, hand-off my legacy to the next generation. In fact all of my staff is a generation younger than me and one of them is young enough to be my grandchild. Wow! When did I get that old? I could fade off into the sunset of irrelevance, but I refuse to do that. My wife and I are getting ready for retirement/reallocation, but we are pressing hard into handing off ourselves significantly and meaningfully to the next generation.

You may wonder what you have to offer, but I am sure that you do have plenty to hand-off. We all do - with or without degrees or dissertations. Unless you have been totally clueless and irresponsible with your living, you have learned a thing or two. And you are likely a step or two ahead of someone. Keeping what you have learned to yourself is presumptuous, self-interested, insecure and inappropriate. Step up and admit what you bring to the table of life and serve it up!

Before we move on, this is one caveat to this first part of offering your expertise. Legacy-leaving is less specific than you'd think. The things you have to offer are more attitudinal, value-based, and strength oriented. They are customized. As you offer your legacy to someone to make their own, it will be a morph of things you offer, things other people offer, circumstances, environment and many other elements. So really, your expertise is not really expertise at all. It is generalities. So before you get offended that your legacy recipient doesn't do exactly as you did, remember this: effective legacy-making has an element of being an expert at not being an expert. You offer your legacy.

Make an Offer - Once we come to terms with what we bring to the table to hand off, we have to offer it to those who could benefit from it. The key here is posturing. Posturing it with humility makes it much more likely to be received, and more than that, to be applied.

This is how I picture offering legacy to other people. I imagine my palms extending out to them - like I have something on my palms - maybe like a silver dollar. With open hands I am offering that silver dollar - an idea, a mantra, a story - to them. I am going to leave it there. As I retreat my open palms, I leave what I have offered. They can take it or leave it. It can fall to the ground, or they can grab onto it. If it falls to the ground, it is ok because it was only an offering - not a demand. I am not forcing it into their pocket. I am not forcing them to spend it. I am not forcing them to add it to the annals of their mind as the most poignant thing they have ever learned. I have nothing to lose or nothing to gain from their taking the silver dollar. Since they don't have the pressure to take it or apply it, they are more likely to take it. Discovery is among the greatest of empowerers[98], so an offering feels much more like it was their own discovery. If they reject the silver dollar, since it was an offering, there is nothing at stake for me - my ego can stay intact, my experience can stay intact, my feelings about them and about myself can stay intact and my story can stay intact. And maybe, they will benefit from the offering.

Be visionary for someone else - Over the years when I have talked to people about passing on legacy by offering vision, two

---

[98] Discovery is among the greatest of empowerers is one of my personal value statements from my Personal Mission/Vision board I have framed and hung in my man cave. I have "offered" this mantra to countless people over the years.

things happen: they get intimidated and they feel presumptuous. Who are they to offer vision to someone else? Isn't offering vision to someone a little (or a lot) presumptuous that you presume to know enough about them to tell them what they could be doing? Doesn't offering vision to someone put you in a place of importance or maybe even dominance? NO! Being visionary for someone else is about legacy - yours and theirs.

You are imagining a different and bigger future for them. You are seeing something in them that could be fostered and grown into something that can make a difference for the long haul for them, their family, their community and the world. That is not being dominant, or self-aggrandizing or self-important. It is imagining a different future for someone sitting across the table from you!

Those two men I shared about earlier offered vision to me over oyster shooters and a men's retreat because they saw something in themselves and something in me that aligned with them and that could be passed on. They offered me a pathway, a different future for me and potentially/hopefully people around me - like I was around them at that moment and season. I am their legacy. Thanks, Jeff! Thanks, Gary.

Learn From Those You Invest In - A common misperception of leaving a legacy is that it requires someone to be an expert and someone else to be a protege' (or a mentee which sounds too much like a breath mint). A mentor has some experience and expertise in a specific area like a plumber and a plumber apprentice. The protege is in a formal cycle of learning, applying and repeating to a point of competency.

Leaving a legacy may be specific and may have some formalities (learning competencies, time frames, key results, etc) like mentoring contains, but it is also general. In fact, it is far less formal because more formality usually translates into less relationship. Legacy-Leaving is relationship based. I like to take it even one step further.

I like to describe our church as a relationship church, rather than a relational church. The difference may seem semantical, but it isn't. Relationship is something you have and something you are. It is a noun. It is an organism with two or more entities who are entwined and interacting. It is vibrant and active.

Being relational is an adjective that describes the noun. By definition, relational is:

> [Concerned with] the way in which two or more people or things are connected. (i.e.,]"Power is a relational concept that can only be understood in terms of interactions between individuals and groups"[99]

Relational describes the connecting, but it isn't the connection. Relational is the verb; the action. Being relational is more behavioral. Relationship is more personal. It is a noun!

Why does this matter when it comes to leaving a legacy? It matters in how it links to the previous section on Making an Offer. Offering legacy is a compelling power, not one that can be demanded. In legacy-making, the one making the offer cannot demand that recipient do it, unless legacy making is commingled with paid supervisory authority when payment can be withheld if the offer is not heeded and enacted. And this makes the offer a demand and can complicate legacy-making. But even a supervisor can make a demand more compelling and less demanding by practicing something I call Reciprocating Relationships.

---

[99] Oxford University Press. Downloaded October 26, 2023.

I am mechanically disinclined and disinterested, so as I describe this next construction tool, bear with me. A reciprocating saw is a saw that cuts by both pushing and pulling. It moves in two directions to accomplish its task - which is demolition and not construction. The demolition most often is done to come alongside the demolished areas and build something in its place.

Legacy-building is like a reciprocating saw. It moves in both directions with the end goal of building something to replace something else. The thing being replaced is usually an inferior, and less than optimum, less effective thing; be it an action, behavior, impression, belief, etc.

In legacy relationships, the dismantling and rebuilding happens to both people in the relationship. It is reciprocating! Anyone who offers a legacy has to be humble enough to receive even more input for their own legacy which is simultaneously being built at the same time it is being given away. In other words - always be a student.

Reciprocating relationships cut both ways. Both people in the relationship are bringing things to the table of life that both people can learn from.

One of the most exciting aspects of my current job as a Lead Pastor is the intentional hand-off I am making to whom I hope will be the next Lead Pastor of our church. A couple of years ago, when I interviewed him, I got insecure. He was confident in his competence. He was young enough to be my son, but he had great experience and had a "get it done" attitude. As attracted as I was to that, I was also a little intimidated. I wasn't sure if I could lead him because he was so strong. We kept talking and I was able to see that though strong, determined and experienced, he was also humble, respectful and teachable. And if I tried to remain humble, respectable and teachable myself, I could see some things he could teach me too. And a few years later, it is working. He is learning. I am learning. He is offering himself to me and I am offering myself to him. And I think parts of my legacy are being handed off and his is too.

COMING FULL CIRCLE

Have you ever wondered where the English word "legacy" comes from. As I was closing out this chapter, and this book, I was wondering. Here is what I tracked down:

> late 14c., legacie, "body of persons sent on a mission," from Medieval Latin legatia, from Latin legatus "ambassador, envoy, deputy," noun use of past participle of legare "send with a commission, appoint as deputy, appoint by a last will"[100]

Originally, legacy had to do with passing on one's wealth and possessions to someone else. This was completed through a third party and was a legal function carried out by a representative(s). Somewhere along the line, it morphed into what I have been talking about, not just in this chapter, but in this whole book.

Cambridge English Dictionary defines legacy as something that is a result of events in the past (e.g., the bitter legacy of a civil war.)

According to Oxford Learner's Dictionaries, legacy can be defined as any amount of money or even property that is left to someone via their last will and testament.

---
[100] https://www.etymonline.com/word/legacy. Visited site November 9, 2023.

The Lexico Dictionary tells us that the word legacy can be used in the technology world as well. Legacy defined here is in reference to hardware or software that has been superseded but, due to its wide use, is difficult to replace

The adjective (or noun) legacy has an additional and much broader definition when it refers to things that are the results of past events. Legacy — pronounced ˈleg·ə·si — is something that is handed down to us from past generations and ancestors alike.[101]

The definition from the Lexico Dictionary excerpt bothers and inspires me a little. That definition speaks of antiquated hardware or software. As I have aged, I have been fighting the feeling and function of being antiquated. As everyone who is aging says, "it happens so fast" and it did for me. There have definitely been times in the last decade where I have had to fight for my relevance.

My last job shift was 90% for that reason. My prior church had what I considered an undue and unbalanced shift to the younger generation. Me and my contemporaries were slowly and regularly shifted to the irrelevant closet. I remember one conversation I had with one of my bosses when I asked him to please start giving me a warning the next time he started to neuter me - as I gave a gesture with my hands resembling scissors making a snip. He knew what I was referring to - you probably should too since I talked about men's lack of being initiators of vision as being impotent.

I was able, by God's grace and guidance, to reallocate my career and my passion to my current church and community - which I love! But also was able to learn that legacy-leaving is not about jobs or careers. It is about relationships and handing off

---

[101] https://thewordcounter.com/meaning-of-legacy/. Visited site November 9, 2023.

bits and pieces of yourself and what you have learned to other people who may benefit from it - with the hopes that their bits and pieces will get handed off to someone else.

As I was in the last couple of chapters of this book, something happened that was beyond my strategic orchestrations - in life and in writing. I was beginning a vacation that involved an Ironman event in Coeur d'Alene, Idaho. My wife had gone to Idaho ahead of me to spend time with her parents. I was driving there with my bike and other triathlon gear. I love road trips with friends and by myself. On this drive I was by myself. As I was driving, I received a voice text from a new friend of mine. His name is Nathan. I have known this man for a long time - since the time he was much younger. And in the last year, we struck up a legacy-relationship. We began meeting for coffee to talk about life and such. We had met only a couple of times when I received this message:

Hey, Carlyle. This message is going to be a little longer, so I didn't feel like texting you because that would be a long text. So, I know you know that on June 19th, on Father's Day, we always go on a family vacation. Something that I noticed is that my relationship with Jesus during the four or five days we were there really dwindled and was almost non-existent. It seems like it was not there at all. I was doing my best to draw near to Him. I was trying to read my Bible a little bit more, and pray a little bit more and think about Him a little bit more. But for some reason it didn't work. But I have noticed that since I have been back it was like "boom", it's back to normal. So I didn't know if you experience that with your relationship with Jesus when you're on vacation. I don't travel very much, so it's not a big thing, but I wondered if you had any tips or suggestions for me for the next time it happens. I'd love to hear them. Talk to you soon.

Here was my text message reply:

Hey, yeah, I experience that sometimes too. I think there could be two very easy reasons for feeling distant. One is it's a weirdly emotional time for you guys. Second, you were with your family pretty much nonstop and away from your normal regimens for spiritual disciplines in your life. So off the cuff, that's what I think was going on. Good job on being aware of it, and wondering about it, and getting to the bottom of it! I have been by myself since Friday, since Tina is in Idaho. So I had a little bit of that as well, even though I was at home. I will tell you about a discovery I felt Jesus led me into when we see each other. I am on the road to Iron Man, Idaho right now!

    I was just thinking also, the role that you still have in your family probably prevents you from focusing on your relationship with Jesus as much as you guard your family and protect them. So that could've been taking some emotional and spiritual energy from you.

Before I composed that reply, I had to compose myself, not because I didn't know what to say, but because of what it meant to me that my friend had reached out to me. This was a full circle legacy moment for me!
    This friend of mine is a second generation friend. Really I was a friend of his dad, and now we are friends. When I say I WAS friends with his dad, it is because his dad and I are not really friends anymore. Well, we are still kinda friends - actually kind of really close, but we are kind of not friends anymore. Sounds complicated, but it's not.

His dad is/was my friend Jon that I started this book telling you about. Jon is my friend who died unexpectedly from a heart attack while on a family vacation. My new friend confiding in me, was there and saw his dad die in front of his eyes. The vacation he was referring to in the message was the annual vacation they take to commemorate their dad - on the anniversary of his death. Talk about an emotionally loaded trip. They do it every year and it really is a celebration of Jon's life and theirs too as they have reconstructed their lives. Here is a picture of Nathan and me just months after his dad died. He was 14 years old then.

I was beginning to forge a relationship with him through triathlon. Like I said, I knew Nathan a long time, since before he was born. But I didn't really know him. We didn't have our own relationship.

Nathan is a man now. He is 21 years old. Since Jon died, we slowly became more acquainted, but it wasn't deep. It wasn't legacy-making. Earlier this year, his grandmother died and I was honored to officiate at her service. After the service, I took a risk and asked him if he would be up for getting coffee so I could hear about some recent developments in his life that his mother - whom my wife and I are still very close to - had mentioned to me. He enthusiastically agreed. So we started meeting.

When Nathan sent me that message, it was a crossroads in our relationship. It was also a crossroads for me. Legacy was happening. I was given the honor and privilege to pour some of my life and his dad's life back into him. And he was eager to take it on. We are still meeting regularly. I love it. I love him - in his own rite - not because he is Jon's son, but because he is Nathan.

What I experience when I am with him is profound. I genuinely enjoy being around him. He is smart, deep, and spiritual. He reminds me of his dad sometimes. He reminds me of his mom sometimes. He reminds me of me sometimes. But he is Nathan.

He is distinct and he is growing. Not just because he is in his early twenties, but because he is open to legacy building and so am I.

I want you to experience that type of legacy-making. It may not be as emotionally loaded and profound as my time with Nathan is, it may not be with a twenty year-old, but giving yourself away is one way you live well past your life and have more impact than you'll probably ever know. Giving yourself away is an honor, it is a privilege, and it is your responsibility. Get off your non-legacy making butt and pour yourself out to someone else. Offer yourself with some grit! Be a gritty friend! You and your friends will be better for it.

> *"Friendship is unnecessary, like philosophy, like art, like the universe itself... it has no survival value; rather it is one of those things which give value to survival."*
>
> C.S. Lewis — 20th Century Religious Philosopher, Author

DISCUSSION QUESTIONS

1. If you could pick some adjectives to describe the legacy you want to leave behind, what would they be?
2. In what ways do you think a man's legacy is different from a woman's?
3. Who has poured legacy into you? How much of that was planned and intentional compared to unplanned and accidental?

4. Do you hesitate to leave a legacy? Do you think of legacy-leaving as an option or a responsibility? Why?
5. Have you ever been surprised by hearing that you left an impact on someone? Was it positive or negative? How did finding that out leave a legacy on you?
6. What can you do to be more intentional about legacy-making?

Made in the USA
Middletown, DE
09 July 2024